The Value of Christ

Kenneth D. Steadman

The Value of Christ by Kenneth D. Steadman

© 2016 by Kenneth D. Steadman. All rights reserved.

Books may be purchased by contacting the author at: **www.John442.com**

Printer: DiggyPOD

Copy edited by Michael LaRocca of MichaelEdits.com. Cover Art by Kevin Pettis

ISBN: 978-0-9989088-0-9

Printed in United States of America

Contents

Jesus Christ as Lord

Thank you to ….

Rev. Cedric H. Jones Jr., who showed me the value of a lifelong friend,

Rev. Dr. Clifton A. Jones, who showed me the value of a called pastor,

Robert and Betty Lee, and **Rev. Brad and Jean Humphrey**, who showed me the value of Christian love,

Rev. Justin Paslay, who showed me the value of a brother in Christ,

Rev. Lorenzo Small, who showed me the value of a few diligent workers,

Marselene Steadman, who showed me the value of a Godly wife.

And a *very special thank* you to

Dr. Eric Eanes, who showed me the value of relevant teaching: that the value of what is taught lies in what is learned.

May God richly bless you all.

To my friend, **Scott Cadmus**: Only 36 years late on the book. Life Happens.

Preface

Does any Believer in Jesus Christ as their Savior and Lord really understand how they came to that decision? I've been going to church a good portion of my life and never heard a valid, non-religious answer. The Value of Christ is an attempt to make the concept of Jesus Christ as Savior and Lord easy to understand. It's not a particularly religious concept. In fact, the book is based on the very logical, everyday concept that runs our lives, Value, choosing one thing over another because it gives more of what we want, without giving up too much of what we already have. While this book is about Christianity, my hope is that it will be considered more about decision-making.

Too often, Christians want non-Christians to convert without knowing (or remembering) the mindset of those they are trying to convert. While we have the Christian duty to "go and make disciples," Jesus also said, "Those who are well have no need of a physician, but those who are sick." Some may think that going to a doctor when healthy is not exactly the best use of their time or money. In this book, cost and benefit, what's "worth it" and what's not, are explained in simple fashion. I'd like to highlight a few points on the style in which this book was written, in hopes they will aid in your understanding.

The Value of Christ is the first in a five-book series, *A Voice from the Congregation*. For too long, "church folk" have left the understanding of God's word to the pulpit. I believe the Bereans of Acts 17:11 had it right; check the Scriptures to know that what you're hearing is true. Too often we follow the pastor rather than following him as *he follows Christ* (1 Corinthians 11:1). Why? Because we do not know Christ for ourselves; therefore, we don't know whether or not the pastor is following Him! It is my hope that, Lord willing, this series will clarify what we in the congregation *should* know and that for which we will be held accountable to God (Deuteronomy 29:29).

Three gentlemen helped me in writing *The Value of Christ*. Each has an evangelistic spirit much stronger than mine. They go out often, sharing the Gospel with folks on an almost daily basis. I noticed that spirit of sharing immediately and decided they would be a good litmus test for what is being shared with the unbelieving world. These guys aren't the ones downtown, standing on the plastic crate, yelling "REPENT, THE END IS NEAR, REPENT!!"

No, these are men of God, who are doing what God has told all Believers to do: "…go and spread the gospel …." They're a little more faithful than most. I wanted them included in this book for one reason; I wanted to see, as evangelists, what they thought vs. what I thought. These three fellas are "boots on the ground" of evangelism. Take what *I* wrote in the light of what *they* wrote.

You might notice quite a few cultural references. Some are from my youth, some from adulthood, some I wasn't around to observe, and some I have not a clue as to how they came to be. If they are dated, so be it. I believe culture is a mix of what is, what was, and what will be. I also believe that, while some may question the context in which the quotes were originally rendered, God weaves Himself into culture in some places we would not think to look for Him.

Last, you will see I often use masculine pronouns when writing. Alas, I am not as politically correct as the world would like. While I mean no offense to any female reader, I also give no apologies. I will add this: The Word of God was/is not gender neutral, no matter how some translations/versions of the Bible would have you believe differently. And while *The Value of Christ* is not holy writ, it is written to give glory to my Lord and Savior, Jesus Christ, as is the Bible. I believe the lack of focus on masculinity has resulted in the weakening of male responsibility in the church, of the church, and cast a veiled view of God's glory. Again, I mean no offense; consider it writer's privilege.

With those three things in tow, may this book bring clarity both to those who know Christ and those who do not.

Ever Forward.

Kenneth D. Steadman

Introduction

"Then what shall I do with Jesus who is called Christ?"

– Matthew 27:22 (NASB)

This question Pontius Pilate raised is the most important question you will ever have to answer. In that answer comes your path in this life and your permanent home in the next. To understand the consequences of your answer, you must be informed about the choices. That's what this book is about, making the right choice *for you*.

The authors believe that this choice should begin with rational, logical thought. The concept of salvation is not mystical; the application of it is. Christ's followers proclaim Him, and unBelievers hear and believe. A spiritual transformation takes a Believer from being a child of Satan to a child of God and obedience to Christ. The spiritual transformation starts with our hearing and comprehending the *truth*.

The truth enlightens the right choice. Perhaps that is why the Merriam-Webster Dictionary provides a definition of Christ as "the ideal truth that comes as a divine manifestation of God to destroy incarnate error."

"Come now, and let us reason together," says the Lord,
"Though your sins are as scarlet, they will be as white as
snow; Though they are red like crimson, they will be like
wool."

– Isaiah 1:18 (NASB)

Why do you choose one thing over another? This car over that one; this cell phone over that one; this menu item over that one? What's the difference? Don't you decide on this one over the others because you believe you will benefit (something that makes you better) from the item you chose more than from the other choices available? This is how we *reason*.

Reasoning is the decision-making process created in Man to let us think through something so that it makes sense. Man's decision-making process was designed to find *value*. What is value? The Oxford Dictionary defines value as a noun:

val·ue [valyo͞o]: the regard that something is held to deserve;
                            the importance, worth, or usefulness of something

and as a verb:

val·ue [valyo͞o]: consider (someone or something) to be
                            important or beneficial; have a high opinion of

Both as a noun and verb, value's definition has something to do with worth or benefit. If we put this definition in equation form, perhaps it would be easier to understand. That equation might look like this *Value Equation*:

$$\textbf{Value = Benefit – Cost}$$

The value of something is equal to the benefit after its cost (something one must give up to obtain the benefit) has been considered. Value is the leftover benefit once you subtract the cost. After all, if it costs more than it's worth, then why buy it? Or if the benefit is equal to the cost, why not find something that will bring you more benefit?

We are willing to pay for what we want because we think the item will be "worth it." When you say, "It's not worth it," aren't you really saying that the *benefit* is not worth the *cost*? By using the concept of value in decision-making, Man has been given a process by which to decide what is in his best interest.

When discussing the value of Christ, God wants neither "warm fuzzy feelings," a bunch of "religion," nor blind obedience. God gave Man a mind to reason so he can understand and make wise decisions. Using the questions associated with the Value Equation to determine value, Christ can easily be evaluated by answering three simple questions.

Question 1: *What is the benefit of Christ?*

Question 2: *What is the cost of Christ?*

Question 3: *Is the benefit greater than the cost?*

If the benefit is greater, then you should "follow" Him. If the cost is greater, then you shouldn't "follow" Him. That's the way Joshua thought in Joshua 24:15 (NASB):

> ***If it is disagreeable in your sight to serve the Lord, choose for yourselves today whom you will serve: whether the gods which your fathers served which were beyond the River, or the gods of the Amorites in whose land you are living; but as for me and my house, we will serve the Lord.***

There's just one small problem. As clean, simple, and objective as our definitions and equation appear, we must consider the subjective matter of opinion. Joshua presents two ways of thinking, of mindset:

1. the "**disagreeable in your sight**" camp

as opposed to

2. the "**as for me and my house**" camp

What might appear beneficial to you might not be worth the cost to me. And what you consider a ridiculous cost, I might think is a relatively small amount. Want to see an example? Let's look at John 3:16 (NIV), which the great German professor of theology, Martin Luther, called "the Gospel in miniature."

For God so loved the world that he gave his one and
only Son, that whoever believes in him shall not perish
but have eternal life.

If we use the three questions that are a part of our Value Equation to find the "true benefit" of the Only Begotten (one and only) Son, HIM, Jesus Christ, we'd ask:

1. *What is the benefit of Christ?* (Believers) shall not perish but have eternal life.

2. *What is the cost of Christ?* You believe in Him.

3. *Is the benefit greater than the cost* (or Is He Worth It)???

That seems to be a matter of opinion:

- God the Father thought so, that's why He "gave" (to die) God the Son, Jesus Christ;

But it was the LORD's good plan to crush him (Jesus)
and cause him grief.

– Isaiah 53:10 (NIV)

- The rich young ruler didn't think so, once he found out what "believes in Him" involved.

…he was saddened, and he went away grieving….

– Mark 10:22 (NASB)

- God the Son, Jesus Christ, thought so; that's why He agreed to be given (to die).

> *I lay down My life so that I may take it again. "No*
> *one has taken it away from Me, but I lay it down on*
> *My own initiative."*
>
> – John 10:17-18 (NASB)

- Some of those who were called Jesus's disciples didn't think so, once they found out what "believes in Him" meant.

> *…many of His disciples withdrew and were not walking*
> *with Him anymore.*
>
> – John 6:66 (NASB)

- The tax collector, Matthew, thought so because he gave up his very lucrative tax collection franchise.

> *And he left everything behind, and got up and*
> *began to follow Him.*
>
> – Luke 5:28 (NASB)

Why do some think Christ is of value, while others do not? Could it be how they define benefit and cost? What unit of measure, what code, what *standard* determines what is beneficial and what is costly? Who decides?

Both groups, those who value Christ and those who do not, agree on what you get and what you give up. However, there is more to it than that. To be truthful, the benefit is more than an eternal lifespan and the cost greater than mere academic agreement.

We must define a standard way of thinking, a particular light, a mindset under which a decision can be reached. Once the standards of benefit and cost are actually determined, then the questions will make more sense. We will talk about this standard throughout our value creation process.

Perhaps you should hold off on deciding if the benefit of following Christ is greater than the cost until you have a little more information and a better-defined standard. In the meantime, let's develop a process to gather, think about, and use the data we need in order to create value. This is also a three-step process:

1. turn data into information (define and collect data that matters, put data into context; turn relevant (or important) data into information)

2. turn information into knowledge (the skill of *how* to use information)

3. turn knowledge into wisdom (the skill of *when* to use knowledge)

On our road to wise decision-making, before we begin to evaluate the value of Christ, let's gather some data and turn it into information.

Jesus Christ as Savior

And I am certain that God, who began the good work within you, will continue his work until it is finally finished on the day when Christ Jesus returns.

– Philippians 1:6 (NLT)

The Creation of Man

In the beginning God created the universe.
– Genesis 1:1 (ISV)

Contained within that sentence of seven words is the foundation for reality. All that exists today outside of God Himself, whether we see it or not, came to be in one moment by way of creation. As the subsequent verses of Genesis Chapter 1 show, God simply speaks and things that didn't exist before come into being "ex nihilo" from nothing. When He spoke, He created not only the finished product but the very material (the matter) that makes up creation.

All things came into being through Him, and apart
from Him nothing came into being that has come
into being.
– John 1:3 (NASB)

This supernatural event is the beginning of all things that we perceive as reality: time, space and matter to be exact. In creation we also have cause and effect, which is God creating reality. An intelligent being imposed His will simply by speaking it into existence. This is reality. Each day that we awake, open our eyes and see, we experience reality. A simple internet search provides the following definition for reality:

"Reality is the state of things as they actually exist, rather than

as they may appear or might be imagined."

In a wider definition, reality includes everything "that is and has been, whether or not it is observable or comprehensible." A still broader definition includes "everything that has existed, exists, or will exist."

In a very simple sense God Himself is reality. Simply put, truth is reality. God is truth. God is reality, and because God is the god of truth, His word is true, as the Bible says time and time again. Genesis 1:1 is the foundation of all Scripture and is the reason why there is a reality as opposed to nothing existing at all.

How does this truth benefit the believer, a follower of Christ? As I stated before, each of us awakens in the morning to reality and at some point in life our minds bring us to ask ourselves: Why am I here (experiencing reality) or what is my purpose in life (the visible part of reality)? For what purpose?

Some say:

> *"In a universe of electrons and selfish genes, blind physical forces and genetic replication, some people are going to get hurt, other people are going to get lucky, and you won't find any rhyme or reason in it, nor any justice. The universe that we observe has precisely the properties we should expect if there is, at bottom, no design, no purpose, no evil, no good, nothing but pitiless indifference."*

– Richard Dawkins,
English ethologist, evolutionary biologist, and author

But what does God tell us?

> *Then God said, "Let Us make man in Our image, according to Our likeness; and let them rule over the fish of the sea and over the birds of the sky and over the cattle and over all the Earth, and over every creeping thing that creeps on the Earth. God created man in His own image, in the image of God He created him; male and female He created them."*

– Genesis 1:26-27 (NASB)

We know that our God is good. God designed us with purpose and set us apart from the other creatures. We were and are to this day different and not just mere byproducts of pond scum that evolved into monkey-men. Knowing that we were intelligently created, the Believer can have faith that God always has a purpose for him, that God always works things for the good of His chosen. We can know that we are not merely victims of time and chance or pitiless indifference.

For since the creation of the world, His invisible attributes,
His eternal power and divine nature, have been clearly seen,
being understood through what has been made, so that they
are without excuse…. For they exchanged the truth of God
for a lie, and worshiped and served the creature rather than
the Creator, who is blessed forever. Amen.

– Romans 1:20,25 (NASB)

– Jonathan D'Mario Williams

In The Beginning.

"I can assure this is the beginning of a meaningful relationship….
That fuss was us!"

– Parliament, *Gloryhallastoopid (Or Pin the Tale on the Funky)*

Then God said, "Let Us make man in Our image, according
to Our likeness…."

– Genesis 1:26 (NASB)

The creation of Man: what an awesome topic! Millions of years in the creation of evolutionary goo that came from some other evolutionary goo, that came from some Big Bang that came from…ahhh…ahhh…nothing? Does anyone question how something can be created without a creator? *Ain't theory grand?*

For the purposes of the truth, I'd rather discuss the creation of Man by his creator, God. So we'll discuss the subject of Man's creation in three parts:

1. Who Created Man?

2. How was Man Created?

3. Why was Man Created?

Now I'd like to believe that if you are reading a book entitled *The Value of Christ*, you will forgive me if I do not take up your precious time (and my costly word count) on debating Evolution vs. Creation. I leave that debate to those who have the gift of debating. I am a simple man writing with other simple men. We speak of what we know and testify of what we have seen. Because we know God and have seen His work, we will, with that claim, state it to be good enough to believe. For the next few pages, please give us the benefit of your doubt that we were created.

In the beginning God created the heavens and the Earth.

– Genesis 1:1 (NASB)

Before we can tackle the deep subject of the creation of Man, we have to cover an even deeper subject, The Creator of Man, God. A. W. Tozer's *Knowledge of the Holy* aids me well in explaining the subject of God:

"What is God like? If by the question we mean,

"What is God like in Himself?" there is no answer."

God is God. He is all-knowing, all-powerful, all…everything! Should one attempt to describe the Creator? Why don't we simply ask God who He is?

> ***But Moses protested, "If I go to the people of Israel and tell***
> ***them, 'The God of your ancestors has sent me to you,' they***
> ***will ask me, 'What is his name?' Then what should I tell them?"***
> ***God replied to Moses, 'I Am Who I Am. Say this to the people***
> ***of Israel: I Am has sent me to you.'***
>   – Exodus 3:13-14 (NLT)

Look, if the only way God can describe Himself is *I Am*, how can I do better? When Man has come to the end of his understanding, he stands at the foot of God. (*I told you this was going to get deep…like Alice in Wonderland's rabbit hole.*) I believe God wishes to explain Himself sufficiently, for our puny understanding, with the first verse in the Bible. ***In the beginning God created the heavens and the Earth.***

God, through His will, creates not only all of the nature (both animate and inanimate) we see here on Earth but all of the universe and its planets, stars, nebulae, and any other feature of the heavens for His own purpose.

The first few verses of the Book of Genesis fully explain the power, creative abilities, goodness, knowledge, etc.… of God. "He created the heavens and the Earth. All that is and all that was, He created." In fact, He spoke, and there it was.

God was before time and space and matter and science and theory and knowledge and being and …Man. And just in case you want God to tell you this Himself, let's quickly look at the Book of Job.

Job was in right standing with God; in fact, at that time he had the best relationship with God of any person on Earth (Job 1:8). Yet when things started going sideways in Job's life, and he wanted to get answers from God, how did God respond? Well…

> *Then the Lord answered Job from the whirlwind: "Who is*
> *this that questions my wisdom with such ignorant words?*
> *Brace yourself like a man, because I have some questions*
> *for you, and you must answer them. "Where were you*
> *when I laid the foundations of the Earth? Tell me, if you know*
> *so much. Who determined its dimensions and stretched out*
> *the surveying line? What supports its foundations, and who*
> *laid its cornerstone as the morning stars sang together and*
> *all the angels shouted for joy? …. Have you ever commanded*
> *the morning to appear and caused the dawn to rise in the east?"*
>
> *– Job 38:1-7,12 (NLT)*

Oh, that's right, Job was on his break during those occurrences—and God goes on and on for about *four* chapters. Get the point? I believe Job did. Would you want to hear the voice of God explaining the creation of the world in *this* tone? I think not.

This is God. You either believe He exists or you don't. You either believe He is responsible for all creation or you don't. Genesis is true, or it isn't. Either way, your opinion has absolutely no effect on the truth. Reality is the state of things as they actually exist, rather than as they might appear or be imagined. God said: "*I Am Who I Am.*"

This is God, who created Man.

Snips and Snails, Sugar and Spice.

"Snips and snails, and puppy dogs[sic] tails, That's what
little boys are made of. Sugar and spice and all things nice,
That's what little girls are made of."
— attributed to Robert Southey, English poet
What Are Little Boys Made Of?

Then the LORD God formed man of dust from the ground,
and breathed into his nostrils the breath of life; and man
became a living being.
— Genesis 1:26 (NASB)

Man was created physically from dust and God's breath. The science of making the physical body of Man made from the dust of the Earth might seem a bit farfetched, but it is what the Bible states (Ecclesiastes 3:20).

Just open up a coffin a few decades after a body has been laid to rest and ask yourself if the lodger was never in there, walked out of there, or if he just turned into "dust." What you see going into the ground is not what you see when you pull it back up after the Earthly body decays. God created Man from the Earth.

"99% of the mass of the human body is made up of the
six elements: oxygen, carbon, hydrogen, nitrogen, calcium,
and phosphorus."
— DataGenetics

What makes Man so special? Is it the "breath of life?" Genesis 2:7 says that God breathed the life into Man. But Genesis 7:15 states that the animals in Noah's Ark had the breath of life in them too. So are we just like the beasts of the field?

Does evolutionary theory have some basis in fact? Well—no. What makes Man different is not what he is on the *outside* so much as what he is on the *inside*.

God made Man in His image and likeness. The great minds of Christianity have thought about just what that means. One of the greatest theologians, Charles Spurgeon, explained it this way:

"All the attributes of Christ, as God and man, are at our disposal.

All the fullness of the Godhead, whatever that marvelous term may comprehend, is ours to make us complete."

What sets Man apart from other animals is that we can "reflect" the attributes of God. The creator can see Himself most fully in Man. Ever heard about a son who has "his father in him?" What that means is the nature of the father has been passed on to the son. But what does *nature* mean? Merriam-Webster Dictionary defines it as:

nature na·ture \'nā-chər\: the character or personality of a person

Imagine a man with the personality of God. Imagine a man who reflects the characteristics of God, a child of God. Have you not heard that Believers are "children of God" (Romans 8:16)?

Adam was the child of God just as a baby is the created likeness of his father. (As I don't find anything in the Bible about *physical* likeness to God, especially because God is a spirit (John 4:24), I'll not go there.) Adam reflected the characteristics of God. He was not a replication of God, not fully, not even near it; however, he reflected those characteristics sufficiently for God to state that only Man was made in His image and likeness. Even a little bit of God is still a part of God.

"The drop of water is of one nature with the boundless ocean...."
> – Alexander MacLaren, Scottish minster

Within this image and likeness is the reason Man was created: for God's glory.

What is the *glory* of God? Let's find out from one of God's encounters with Moses. You know, Moses, of the Ten Commandments, the parting the Red Sea? If not, read the Book of Exodus (or download Cecil B. DeMille's movie The Ten Commandments...or wait till next Easter and it will be aired in every city in North America). Moses wanted an intimate relationship with God. He wanted to *know* God. He felt the best way to do that was for God to show him His glory (Exodus 33:13-18).

Show and Tell.

"A slave stood behind the conqueror holding a golden crown
and whispering in his ear a warning: that all glory is fleeting."
> – General George C. Patton

Now therefore, I pray You, if I have found favor in Your
sight, let me know Your ways that I may know You, ...
Then Moses said, "I pray You, show me Your glory."
> – Exodus 33:13 &18 (NASB)

To know God's "ways," His course of life or mode of action, is impossible for Man. Our limited minds cannot comprehend a limitless God. Therefore, God shows Moses his *goodness*. Cambridge Bible for Schools and Colleges defines goodness as:

"a spectacle of outward beauty as a visible sign of His moral perfection."

How can Man sum up the perfection of God? As we read above, God reveals Himself through His attributes. In fact, before The Fall and until Jesus, there was no better reflection of God's glory than Adam. God didn't make a bunch of prototypes, just two: Adam and Jesus. Adam was the physical prototype, and Jesus the spiritual. (But we'll get into that more later.) God gave us just a glimpse of His perfection in the creation of Adam. A more perfect example was Jesus Christ. But there is a simpler understanding of God's perfection.

If the concept of His glory is over your head, try the much simpler explanation of God's perfection and the creation of Man found in Psalm 115:3 (NLT):

Our God is in heaven and does whatever He pleases.

Now think on that for a minute:

Whatever He pleases.

Whatever pleases Him.

Whatever.

That's what He does; whatever He wants to do.

No other being has ever existed who can say that. Sure, we have people who say that, maybe even you. *Can't nobody tell ME what to do!* But don't those people eventually end up being…you know…*dead*? Was that their original plan; "I'm going to do what I want to do and then die?" Look, if I could do whatever *I* wanted, why in the world would I *not* want to live forever?

Unfortunately for the self-created, self-propelled, and self-sufficient, sooner or later they realize they cannot sustain their own delusions. Never have, never will. The only self-sufficient being is God. He needs nothing else because *He* is All.

Now imagine the Creator and Maintainer of all things in the universe, Mr. Perfect, wants as His good pleasure, for you to have a right relationship with Him. Can you imagine being perfectly created to have a relationship with a perfect Father, reflecting the perfect attributes of a perfect God, living in a perfect world? (Yeah, you're right; I can't imagine it, either.) That was the position Adam and Eve were in while in paradise. They lived not just in location, but in mind and relationship in paradise.

Hold the Onions.

> *"Not zucchini, fettuccini, or bulgur wheat, But a big warm*
> *bun and a huge hunk of meat. Cheeseburger in paradise.*
> *Heaven on Earth with an onion slice...."*
>
> – Jimmy Buffet, *Cheeseburger in Paradise*

> *And the Lord God planted a garden in Eden, in the east, and*
> *there he put the man whom he had formed. And out of the*
> *ground the Lord God made to spring up every tree that is*
> *pleasant to the sight and good for food.*
>
> – Genesis 2:8-9 (ESV)

We can infer that Adam and Eve walked with God in the Garden of Eden in the cool of the day (Genesis 3:8). Why? Just as you have to spend some time with someone to get to know them, God wanted Man, Adam and Eve, to spend some time with Him, so that they might know *Him*. On one of my favorite Christian Web sites, *CARM.org* (*Christian Apologetics & Research Ministry*), Matt Slick writes:

"What does it mean for God to walk with them? It means closeness, intimacy, communion. Picture this. Adam and Eve and God literally walking next to each other in perfect harmony. Why did God walk with them? Because He loved them. Because He wanted fellowship with them."

So God, the proud Father, is walking with His children. Seeing Himself in them, even in a very, very, very, very...small way, He must have thought His creation was ***very good*** (Genesis 1:31). Whether for God the Father or God the Son (or God the Holy Spirit, for that matter), Man was created to have a relationship with God. However, that relationship was based on Man reflecting certain characteristics; one in particular, *holiness*.

holy ho·ly \ˈhō-lē\: religious and morally good

– Merriam-Webster Dictionary

God has a standard. Perfection. God does not walk with you if He does not see you as perfect. Adam and Eve were perfect. God made them perfect. And when they walked with Him, they were perfect. They were perfectly obedient. This is the way God judges perfection in Man: if you obey Him on every occasion and in total. *No exceptions, no excuses*. Either He sees your perfect obedience to Him, or He does not consider you to have obeyed Him at all.

He created a lush, fertile paradise for us to enjoy with Him. Granted, the world we live in now is a fallen, pre-apocalyptic nightmare in comparison to the *very* good state the Lord finished it on Day 6. But truly, is *He* to blame for that? Or is it, once again, that the truth was before us and we allowed the Father of Lies (John 8:44) to turn our hearts from the truth and be led astray? As the apostle Paul wrote to the Romans:

For since the creation of the world His invisible attributes,
His eternal power and divine nature, have been clearly
seen, being understood through what has been made, so
that they are without excuse…. For they exchanged the
truth of God for a lie, and worshiped and served the
creature rather than the Creator, who is blessed forever.
Amen.

– Romans 1:20 & 25 (NASB)

And this perfection, this likeness and image, this oneness with God, was all destroyed because of *one* act of disobedience. That is what we call The Fall of Man.

The Fall of Man

In Genesis 3, we can see the benefit of Christ from two different viewpoints—what could have been and what is. The setting is the fruitful, pleasant garden that God created for the Man and the Woman, whom God created in His likeness, for relationship, and with the mandate to fill, subdue, and rule the Earth. The only limit God put on the Man and Woman was that they could not eat from the tree of the knowledge of good and evil.

Into this setting, we saw a new and dangerous character enter: the Serpent. He approached the Woman and asked, "Did God really say, 'You shall not eat of any tree in the garden'?" Here the Serpent questioned God's goodness and implied that God was keeping something good from the Woman.

Eve responded with the penalty for breaking God's promise: "[We should] not eat of the fruit of the tree...so that we may not die." The Serpent, wily as he was, denied this truth and told a partial truth. "You shall not die [a bold-faced lie], but you shall be like God [a partial truth. They would learn the difference between good and evil because they had become evil by defying God]."

Eve was deceived and ate the fruit. Then Adam, who was and had been with her [while the Serpent tempted Eve], ate of the fruit, and they become aware of their inadequacy. They attempted to cover their nakedness, which they did not recognize until after they sinned, to hide themselves from God.

Sin tarnished the image of God in which Adam and Eve have been created. The bearing (in childbirth) of the likeness of God that Adam and Eve were tasked with thus became painful for Eve. Sin tarnished not only Adam and Eve, but all their descendants as well.

It is here that we saw Adam and Eve's need for deliverance, for redemption. God questioned them and provided covering—at the cost of an animal's life. God cursed them and expelled them from the perfect Garden.

Yet there is hope. God extended the benefit of his mercy even in their sin. From Adam and Eve's offspring, a Savior came. This Savior was able to cover the sin of Adam and Eve and all their offspring. What is more, He restored relationship, fellowship, and purpose to mankind. This is the benefit found in Christ."

– Nathan Foth

"Who's Runnin' Thangs?"

> *"The time for honoring yourself will soon be at an end."*
>
> – Maximus, *Gladiator* (2000)

> *"God knows that your eyes will be opened as soon as you eat it,*
> *and you will be like God...."*
>
> – Genesis 3:5

The Fall of Man. You might have heard of it. The Fall of Man is about Man's disobedience to God's singular command and the consequences of this disobedience. But before we dive in, let's get to the question you're probably asking: "From where did Man fall?" Well, in order to get to the fall of *Man*, we have to start with the being who got the ball rolling, Lucifer, also called Satan. You might know him as *the Devil*.

What does the Devil have to do with this? In the deception of Man, the Devil plays a critical role based on the Devil's fall. Let's focus in on the Devil, shall we? Ezekiel 28:12-14 (NLT) describes Satan. This passage is referring to the King of Tyre (but really referring to Satan):

> *You were the model of perfection, full of wisdom and*
> *exquisite in beauty...Your clothing was adorned with*
> *every precious stone—red carnelian, pale-green peridot,*
> *white moonstone, blue-green beryl, onyx, green jasper,*
> *blue lapis lazuli, turquoise, and emerald—all beautifully*
> *crafted for you and set in the finest gold. They were given*
> *to you on the day you were created. I ordained and anointed*
> *you as the mighty angelic guardian.*

As described in this passage, Satan was really something! He was a great angel, created by God, a perfect creation. But not only was Satan a perfect creation, he was given access to God Himself.

> *You had access to the holy mountain of God and walked*
> *among the stones of fire.*

Satan was walking around in the bejeweled home of God!! He was a really, *really* big deal. That is, until verses 15-16 (NLT):

> *You were blameless in all you did from the day you were*
> *created until the day evil was found in you. Your rich*
> *commerce led you to violence, and you sinned.*

So Satan was perfect, without any wrongdoing. But God had to throw Satan out of Heaven.

> *So I banished you in disgrace from the mountain of God.*
> *I expelled you, O mighty guardian, from your place among*
> *the stones of fire.*

Why was Satan evicted? Not because he didn't pay his rent, but because he started reading his own press clippings, drinking the Kool-Aid, believing his own hype, or whatever term your generation applies to him becoming *proud*.

> *Your heart was filled with pride because of all your beauty.*
> *Your wisdom was corrupted by your love of splendor.*

This was the fall of Satan. From a place of great prominence to a place of disgrace, Satan started believing that He was *all that*. In fact, in Isaiah 14:13-14 (NLT), The King of Babylon is described in terms of Satan's corrupted mind:

> *For you said to yourself, "I will ascend to heaven and*
> *set my throne above God's stars. I will preside on the*
> *mountain of the gods far away in the north. I will climb*
> *to the highest heavens and be like the Most High."*

"I will be like the Most High"? Yep, Satan said he was going to be like GOD! Can you imagine, something created stating that it was the Creator? It's kinda like what would happen if I had told my momma I was just as good as she, smart as she, important as she. "Why can't I run things around this house?" (It's hard for me to even write this today without wanting to go hide under my bed.) See why God had to dismiss Satan?

This is the fall of Satan, from perfection to damnation, from having it all to having nothing. From being in a right relationship with the greatest force there is to being everything God hates. This fallen angel is the entity that found its way inside the serpent in the Garden of Eden; this puffed-up, prideful being that hated God because God threw him out of Perfection for getting the big head and thinking he was equal to God Himself. And this is the perfect backdrop to begin the discussion of The Fall of Man. It starts with deception.

Sounds Like a Winner.

> *"All warfare is based on deception."*
> – Sun Tzu, *The Art of War*

> **"Let no one deceive you with empty words, for because of**
> **these things the wrath of God comes upon the sons of**
> **disobedience."**
>
> – Ephesians 5:6 (NASB)

The art of sales is not providing something that's needed, but making one believe one actually needs something. Once your potential customer believes he has a need, then it comes down to having that need met. A great salesman makes you think you're getting that perceived need met, a great benefit, at an unbelievably low cost.

The greatest salesman can make you believe his claim, even if it's not true. Let's see how the greatest salesman of all time, Satan, pulled off the greatest sales pitch of all time.

> **"Did God really say 'you shall not eat of any tree in the garden'?"**
>
> – Genesis 3:1 (ESV)

Eve ate the fruit. Eve told Adam to eat the fruit, and Adam ate the fruit. Nowhere in the Bible does it say that Adam was deceived. It does, however, say that Eve was deceived.

> **And it was not Adam who was deceived by Satan. The**
> **woman was deceived, and sin was the result.**
>
> – 1 Timothy 2:14 (NASB)

> **But I fear that somehow your pure and undivided**
> **devotion to Christ will be corrupted, just as Eve was**
> **deceived by the cunning ways of the serpent.**
>
> – 2 Corinthians 11:3 (NASB)

So what exactly was this *deception* about? It grew from a battle that has been going on since Satan was thrown out of Heaven. Satan hates that he got booted, and he wants to get back at God where he thinks it will hurt. He wants to corrupt God's greatest creation on Earth, the one that most reflects God's attributes, Man. And what better way for Satan to get back at God than to get this great creation to think like Satan; think like him who was cast out by the Creator, rather than to think like the Creator Himself?

Why didn't Satan go after Adam? The Bible doesn't say. Satan deceived Eve. So let's look at that. Why does this deception come so easily to Satan? Because it was based on his own history.

1. Both Satan and Man were created as perfect by God.

2. Both Satan and Man were placed in the best possible situations.

3. Satan was going to use the same thinking to corrupt Man as he had thought when he became corrupted.

But before Satan could tempt Eve, he first had to get her to *mistrust* God. And how to do that? Well, it involved asking simple questions requiring interpretation.

Are you sure *that's* what God said?

"Did God really say you must not eat the fruit from any of the trees in the garden?"

And is what He said *really* what He meant?

"You won't die!"

And if that's what He meant. Is that good for *you*?

"God knows that your eyes will be opened as soon as you eat it, and you will be like God, knowing both good and evil."

Then, as now, Satan wanted Man *not* to understand the will of God.

"She decided that Satan was telling the truth and she had misunderstood
God, but she didn't know what she was doing."
– John MacArthur Study Bible

But let's not put this all on Satan, for he did not get Eve to do anything she didn't want to do. Eve's desire to fulfill the pride in herself was the true problem. Why do I say that? It's summed up in the three lusts of the world:

For the world offers only a craving for physical pleasure,
a craving for everything we see, and pride in our achievements
and possessions. These are not from the Father, but are
from this world.
– 1 John 2:16 (NLT)

She saw that the tree was beautiful and its fruit looked
delicious, and she wanted the wisdom it would give her.
– Genesis 3:6 (NLT)

1. *a craving for everything we see*: She saw that the tree was beautiful, and

2. *a craving for physical pleasure*: its fruit looked delicious, and

3. *pride in our achievements and possessions*: she wanted the wisdom it would give her.

As we see through Eve's actions, sin starts in the mind. Thinking on something that we aren't supposed to think on, lingering there. *Hmmm, beautiful tree… hmmm, fruit looks delicious…. hmmm, I'll know what God knows….*

> *Temptation comes from our own desires, which entice*
> *us and drag us away. These desires give birth to sinful*
> *actions. And when sin is allowed to grow, it gives birth*
> *to death.*
>
> – James 1:14-15 (NLT)

When we take our minds off what *God* wants us to think about and keep it on what our *disobedient nature* wants to think about, we are "dragged away." This is the formula Satan uses in the world today, and he perfected it by using Eve as his first experiment. As we see by Eve's response, Satan was quite successful.

"Is That What Your Momma Taught You?"

> *"My mama told me there'd be lots of guys who look at me and*
> *start to makin' eyes. And then they squeeze and wanna hold*
> *you tight. And say they love you both-a day and night. And*
> *so ya (better be careful hon)."*
>
> – Barbara Lewis, *My Mama Told Me*

> *Train up a child in the way he should go; even when he is*
> *old he will not depart from it.*
>
> – Proverbs 22:6 (NASB)

Have you ever heard that phrase? "Is that what your momma taught you?" Probably not, as the audience for this book were fine, upright tykes in their youth. However, as *I* was an irritant then (and some would ask "What's changed?"), I was asked that question quite often. It's as if just because your momma taught you something, and you *knew* it, you were obligated by pinky-swear to actually *do* it.

In fact, I understood perfectly about knowledge (the understanding of what to do) and wisdom (the understanding of when to do). It goes something like this:

"Ignorance doesn't know; stupid knows, but doesn't do."

Why couldn't the grown-up class simply understand that I was just STUPID (*...makin' momma proud*)? *They should've, 'cause stupid been around a long, long time 'fore I was born.* I'm in the long line of stupid people, starting with Adam and Eve.

"...she took some and ate it. She also gave some to her husband, who was with her, and he ate it."
– Genesis 3:6 (NIV)

The third leg in the three lusts of Man, this ***pride of life***, controls everything else. By disobeying God, and going her own way, Eve was saying that she knew what was best for her, not God. She had gained information sufficient to make a decision about her life and she should be allowed to do what was in her best interest. In short, she should have the same mindset as Satan: "I will be like the Most High."

I will be…like God. This attitude is behind *disobedience*, what we refer to as *sin*. This is the will of Man, to go his own way and to do what is best in his own eyes. Pride works like that. *What can God give us that we cannot get for ourselves? Why should I obey Him? I'm smart. I'm good.*

I'm important (*I'm arrogant* is what we should be thinking). Aren't those attributes what you want to hear today? Isn't that what the world is saying to you today? But why does the world say these things? Because Satan runs this world.

While it is true that God gave Man dominion over this world, Man continually gives control to Satan by obeying the Devil and not God. Satan controls the world today because Man obeys *him* rather than *God*.

"Man was given dominion over the Earth to be vice-regents for God, that is, vice kings to represent God's reign on this planet. Of course, we made a terrible mess out of it, and we were subjected more and more to the power of Satan. Has Satan been given dominion over the Earth until Jesus returns? If so, why was he given this authority…?"

– R.C. Sproul, American theologian, author, and pastor

It's as if Man is Satan's slave. Man is pulling the trigger, but Satan is calling the shots. And Man loves this false sense of control. Satan whispers to the desires within you, "It's OK, you are master of your own destiny. You are your own God." But it's a lie. Man is not in full control. He is being led, one way or another.

Don't you realize that you become the slave of whatever you choose to obey? You can be a slave to sin, which leads to death, or you can choose to obey God, which leads to righteous living.

– Romans 6:16 (NLT)

Hey, but wait a minute. How is it that Eve is deceived but not Adam? Did she just give it to him and he ate it? Didn't he know what God had said? Yep, and he ate the fruit anyway. Go figure. This is why sin came through Adam's disobedience. He was not deceived, there was no misunderstanding. There was just plain, "OK, give it here. I'll eat it."

Therefore, just as through one man sin entered into the world, and death through sin, and so death spread to all men, because all sinned….

– Romans 5:12 (NASB)

It doesn't say "when Eve sinned," it says ADAM. And while deception does not prevent God's punishment, the point here is that God clearly told Adam to obey Him and he clearly said (through his actions) NO! This is the greatest slap in the face Man can give God: disobedience. The created thinking it's the Creator (Romans 1:25). The clay thinking it's the potter (Isaiah 45:9). Man thinking he knows the secret way and will of the all-powerful, all-knowing, all-seeing, all…-EVERYTHING God. But Man finds out the hard way that actions have consequences.

For the wages of sin is death….

– Romans 6:23 (NASB)

Mistake? Yeah. Right.

"There are no mistakes. The events we bring upon ourselves, no matter how unpleasant, are necessary in order to learn what we need to learn…."

– Richard Bach, American writer

"…you must not eat from the tree of the knowledge of good and evil, for when you eat from it you will certainly die."

– Genesis 2:17 (NIV)

Can we get real on the subject of mistakes? "There's no such thing as a mistake if you learned from it." Yeah. Right. Raise your hand if you'd rather make mistakes so you could learn. Here's a thought: maybe you could just trust in what you were taught, and not make the mistake in the first place. We glamorize experience *waaaaay* too much. It shouldn't take you getting your eye put out to know it's not a good idea to run in the house with a pencil in your hand. Case in point, the First Couple, Adam and Eve.

Eve ate the fruit. Adam ate the fruit. God found out they had disobeyed (sinned), and He struck them dead on the spot. Right? Ahhh…no. Not that He couldn't have; perhaps justice demands he *should* have. So then what, death?

> *"When Adam disobeyed, he experienced immediate spiritual*
> *death, which caused him to hide from Lord God among the*
> *trees of the garden. Later, Adam experienced physical death."*
>
> – GotQuestions.org, Question:
> *"What does the Bible say about death?"*

The Bible states there are two deaths: one is involuntary, the physical. The other is voluntary, the spiritual.

> *And inasmuch as it is appointed for men to die once*
> *and after this comes judgment....*
>
> – Hebrews 9:27 (NASB)

When Adam sinned, the connection, the perfect relationship he had with God, died. Of course the obvious goodies went away. God allowing Adam to work without frustration? See ya. Living in the garden of perfection? Adios. No more free lunch. But much more important than that, Adam (and Eve and everyone after them) lost that *closeness* with God. This closeness comes through in Genesis 3:8-10 (NLT):

> *When the cool evening breezes were blowing, the man*
> *and his wife heard the Lord God walking about in the*
> *garden. So they hid from the Lord God among the trees.*
> *Then the Lord God called to the man, "Where are you?"*
> *He replied, "I heard you walking in the garden, so I hid.*
> *I was afraid because I was naked."*

Adam knew what God sounded like walking in the garden because he had heard Him before. And he hadn't hidden the other times because he was not afraid. Why? Because Adam had walked with God in the cool evening breezes. God and Adam had a relationship. As is often said about God and obedient Man, Adam was God's child. Adam and Eve were God's son and daughter. But with that one sin, a single act of disobedience, that perfect relationship was gone for them and all of mankind.

Adam's death was in his spiritual connection to God, the one that is kept only through perfect obedience. That is both how powerful and how fragile our relationship with God is. Perfect obedience can put Man in a relationship greater than he could ever imagine. And all it takes is *one* act of disobedience to destroy it. With that sin, the spiritual part of Adam that connected with the Spirit of God died. Adam's physical death took 930 years (Genesis 5:5); his spiritual death was immediate. You might ask, "But what's that got to do with me?"

Remember that little verse about the wages of sin being death? Well, separation from God does not merely apply to *this* life. That judgment dictates that separation from life with God leads to Man being judged. And because God had already told Adam the sentence (death) for being convicted of the crime of sin, God carries it out both physically and spiritually. Physically, Man will decay until he returns to the dust from which he came. Spiritually, Man will spend eternity separated from God. That's called HELL; maybe you've heard of it?

> *That is the way it will be at the end of the world. The*
> *angels will come and separate the wicked people from*
> *the righteous, throwing the wicked into the fiery furnace,*
> *where there will be weeping and gnashing of teeth.*
> — Matthew 13:49-50 (NLT)

That *fiery furnace* is Hell. And dude, if God sees you as a sinner, you are the very definition of wicked (and for the record, I don't know what ***gnashing of teeth*** is. I don't even want to look it up, *but I know it ain't good*). So Adam really did us a favor, didn't he?

But don't badmouth Adam too much because I (or you) would have done the same thing! It's just who we are as humans: willful, prideful, and ignorant. After all, every person on the face of the Earth came from Adam. Like father, like great, great, great, great, great, etc... grandchildren (Romans 5:12).

So this is our legacy from Adam. Separated from God. Left to our own devices (with great assistance from our worldly advisor, Satan). Put out of Eden. Women suffer pain in childbirth; Men feel frustration and sweat in work. Husband and wife struggle for power. We all are surrounded in a decaying world, wanting this whole train wreck to come to an end. This is where Man was. This is why they call it The Fall, from what Man started out as to what Man became.

But God....

Yet there is hope—God extends the benefit of his mercy even in their sin.

The Reconciliation of Man

Reconciliation. Not many people use reconciliation in daily conversation. If you are familiar with the word reconciliation, you likely heard this word in regard to balancing checkbooks and bank statements, or you might be familiar with its Biblical use. Either way, I believe that not many people know the dictionary definition of reconciliation and don't completely understand the Biblical concept either. So what is the definition of reconciliation?

According to Merriam-Webster, reconciliation is the act of causing two people or groups to become friends again after an argument or disagreement. A good story that displays the idea of reconciliation can be found in Luke 15:11-32.

Consider this paraphrase. Many years ago, a man had two sons. One day, the youngest son demanded his inheritance from his father. (In this time and culture, this demand from son to father was extremely offensive and disrespectful. Simply put, the son was stating that he wished that his father was dead and that he no longer wanted to be the man's son). The father gave his son his portion and the son turned his back on his father and home and went far away.

Not long after, the son lost all of his money. The son recklessly spent all he had on gambling, hookers and drugs. Unfortunately, a huge drought and famine occurred. He had nowhere to live and nothing to eat, so he got a job feeding pigs. He didn't have anything to eat, so he ate whatever was given to the pigs. While with the pigs, he remembered the times when he lived with his father.

He remembered when he had plenty to eat and a place to sleep, that even the servants of his father ate well and were well taken care of. The son decided to go back to his father and humbly ask for a job as a servant because he was no longer worthy to be called a son of his father.

As the son walked down the street toward his home, his father saw him from the porch. His father felt compassion for his son because he deeply loved his son. The father ran to the son with open arms and tears streaming down his face. The son said to his father, "I have hurt you and I have disgraced you. I am no longer worthy to be your son. I am so sorry."

The father told his son that all is forgiven and forgotten. The father told his servants to bring out the best clothes for his son and to prepare a huge party in order to celebrate his son's return. The father declared that his son was dead but is now alive, was lost but is now found.

This parable of the Prodigal Son presents a clear and simple example of reconciliation, from the destruction to the restoration of their relationship. In order for two parties to be reconciled with each other, they first had to have a good relationship. The father and the son above had a good relationship, but the disrespectful and disgraceful actions of the son destroyed their relationship. The son later went to his father in humility after realizing that he had wronged his father.

The father, instead of acting out of judgment or revenge, accepted his son with love, compassion and ultimately forgiveness. Through the son's humility and apology, and through the forgiveness of the father, the relationship that the son and father had before was restored. This is the concept of reconciliation.

This story is an illustration of the reconciliation between God and us. Before Adam and Eve disobeyed God, we had a perfect relationship with God. From that time until now, everyone has been disgracing and disobeying God. This is called sin. Colossians 1:21 states that we are alienated from God, are hostile toward Him, and our actions are evil. God created us for His purposes, yet we are living for ourselves.

Maybe you are wondering how a relationship between us and God can be reconciled and restored. How can we do anything to reconcile with God? The answer is that we can do nothing to reconcile our relationship with God. Only God can reconcile the relationship with us. He must initiate the reconciliation. So you might now be wondering how to know when God initiates reconciliation.

The merciful answer to that question is that God has already initiated reconciliation with us! God has provided a mediator between us and Him. This mediator is God's son, Jesus. From our actions against God, we deserve great punishment and death. However, Jesus took all God's judgment for us in order that we would be reconciled with God.

The only way to be reconciled with God is through Jesus. Without Jesus, we will never be reconciled to God, because as Matthew 7:23 reads, God will say to those who are not reconciled, "I never knew you; depart from me…." We are reconciled with God through God's will, forgiveness, and our obedience to Him. It was God's plan to reconcile with us through Jesus by forgiving all that we had done to disobey and disgrace God.

It doesn't matter what you have done or how long you have done it. God reaches out to you in love and forgiveness. He wants a relationship with you, with all of Mankind. In order to be reconciled with God we need to go back to him humbly and apologetically.

Why does God want to be reconciled with us? Why doesn't God want to judge us so that we get what we deserve? The answer to these questions is that God desires us! He delights in bringing us back into a right relationship with Him. God also wants to reconcile with us for our own good, that we would be with Him instead of suffering eternal punishment. God loves us so much. And because of this love, He has compassion for us and will forgive everything we have done to Him if we accept His gift of eternal life and commit to follow Him. Just like the father forgave his Prodigal Son and celebrated his son's return with a huge party, God also rejoices when we come back to Him.

The reality of God sending His son in my place and every other person's place is mind blowing! I cannot fathom the love that God has for us. His is the kind of love that would stop at nothing in order that we may have a relationship with Him.

I look at everything I have done that is offensive to God, every time I spit in His face by disobeying Him, and I am amazed that He still loves me and that He reached out to me. I am ecstatic that my relationship with God is reconciled. I see the value of restoring my relationship with God. Do you?

– Bradley Wright

Thanks, We've Got It from Here.

"If I could maybe I'd give you my world. How can I when you won't take it from me? You can go your own way, go your own way."

– Fleetwood Mac, *Go Your Own Way*

There is a way that seems right to a man, but its end is the way to death.

– Proverbs 14:12 (NASB)

We humans do what we want, not what is always in our best interest. Why do you think that is? Could it be that we believe that we actually *know* what's best for us? We know the future and what effect it will have on both then and now? Or is that what California Psychics is for? (*You'd think if these guys could tell the future, they'da made enough money not to charge ya, right?*) Scoff if you want. Adam and Eve thought *they* knew what was best for them. Let's gain some knowledge from their situation.

Adam and Eve were just like sinners (those who disobey God) are today. They wanted to do what they wanted to do. They told God, "My will, not yours, be done." This has been the mindset of Man since The Fall. We, like Adam and Eve, do not wish to obey the standard God set, living in total obedience to Him. Instead, we each make our own set of rules, do what we think is best for ourselves, replace the truth of God with the lies we get from Satan, this world, or most often, our own pride.

…every man did that which was right in his own eyes.

– Judges 21:25 (NASB)

Just as the Prodigal Son was allowed to leave, just as Adam was allowed to disobey, God gave us the freedom of our will to go our own way and do our own thing. But at what cost? The loss of paradise? The end of a relationship with the greatest power that exists, the God who created heaven and Earth and—Man?

This is the God who knows all, can do all, and cared (and still cares) about the plight of Man, of *your* eternal fate. But before we get all weepy about how much God cares for you, let's get one thing straight. God is the God of many attributes, none of which are any greater than the other.

God is all *justice* (giving what you rightly deserve) and all *mercy* (not giving you the punishment you rightly deserve) and all *grace* (getting a pardon that you don't rightly deserve) all at once. Don't ask me how; that's a "God" thing.

> **The LORD our God has secrets known to no one. We are**
> **not accountable for them....**
>
> – Deuteronomy 29:29 (NLT)

So when God says you disobey, you die, He means it. He meant it then, and He means it now. God does not change (that's called *immutable*). God in the Garden had the same mindset as He does now. So although He loves Man, He can't go against what He said to Adam, "If you eat its fruit, you are sure to die." So why didn't God strike Adam (and Eve) dead right then and there? For the same reason God doesn't immediately strike dead every sinner who disobeys Him; He is a *merciful* God.

Our Creator wanted to have a relationship with the perfectly obedient Adam, not the prideful, willfully disobedient, sin-natured Adam. The latter Adam, who wanted to listen to Satan and to replace God's will for his life with his own, is not pleasing to God.

But God can't have a relationship with a corpse, and He can't go back on His word. So what was He to do? He created *reconciliation* between himself and Man.

"Oops! My Bad."

> *"The acknowledgment of our weakness is the first step in*
> *repairing our loss."*
>
> – Thomas Kempis, Dutch priest and author

> *For everyone has sinned; we all fall short of God's glorious*
> *standard.*
>
> – Romans 3:23 (NLT)

In the Parable of the Prodigal Son, the son went back to his father when he came to his senses (Luke 15:17). Isn't that an interesting phrase, *came to his senses*? Almost as if there is something called "common sense" (which is, today, neither common, nor sensible), which is the concept of coming in out of the rain, drinking the water you've been led to, or not taking your well water for granted.

It's using the brain God gave Man to see a simple solution to a simple problem. In medical school, they have a thought created by Dr. Theodore Woodward, professor at the University of Maryland School of Medicine:

"When you hear hoofbeats, think of horses not zebras."

How did Adam and Eve use their common sense? Let's take a peek.

As we read above, Adam and Eve ate the fruit, and from the knowledge gained found out they were naked and hid themselves from God. They were ashamed of their nakedness, unlike earlier in Genesis 2:25 when they walked around naked and weren't ashamed.

"For shame implies a sense of guilt, which they did not have,
and an exposedness[sic] to the searching eye of a condemning
judge, from which they were equally free."

– Albert Barnes, American theologian and pastor

What happened? God made Man with a human body that held a spirit. The spirit is the part of Man that sets itself on the things of God. When he was created, Adam thought in line with the way God thought and wished only to be pleasing to Him; all good, all the time. But when Adam sinned, he lost that spirit because it died. The spirit that made Adam most like God, created the desire to be like Him through obedience to Him died and has remained dead in Man to this day.

When Adam ate the fruit, he realized he had disobeyed God and that he was guilty of sin. This guilt showed up in his mind as his nakedness. So he covered himself with fig leaves and hid from, as pastor and theologian Albert Barnes put it, "the searching eye of a condemning judge." Adam hid from the God who walked with him and the friendship they had. God was the source of Adam's peace. But Adam no longer wanted to have a relationship with God!

God looked for him, much like the father looked for his wandering son in the parable. But Adam was ashamed of his actions and his disobedience, yet not so ashamed as to admit it.

When God confronted Adam about disobeying his command, did Adam take responsibility for his disobedience? No, he did what any married man would do —he blamed his wife.

The man said, "The woman whom You gave to be with
me, she gave me from the tree, and I ate."

– Genesis 3:12 (NASB)

Not only did he directly blame Eve, but he indirectly blamed God ("the woman *You* gave me")!! For a perfect God to hear Man blame Him for *his* disobedience, his sin, has got to be hard for God to take. But it wasn't just Adam who had this nerve. Eve didn't want to take the rap either; in the very next verse, Genesis 3:13 (NLT), she passed the blame, as well.

> **Then the LORD God asked the woman, "What have you done?" "The serpent deceived me," she replied. "That's why I ate it."**

Aren't we the same today? What's the reason for *your* situation? How many people, things, or events have you blamed for *your* poor decisions? I'm sure some of you even blame (or have blamed) God. I know I have, and more than once!

At least you know now where this condition of not taking responsibility for your actions came from. Adam might have confessed (half-heartily), but had he repented? *Did Adam 'fess up and say "My Bad. This is on me"?* This pitiful sight sets the stage for Man to "come to his senses" and return to God and believe Him.

When Sorry Won't Cut It.

> *"How can you mend a broken man? How can a loser ever win?*
> *Please help me mend my broken heart and let me live again."*
>   – Rev. Al Green, *How Can You Mend A Broken Heart*

> *"Repent and believe the good news!"*
>   – Mark 1:15 (HCSB)

We are going to talk about *repentance*; changing one's mind, coming to one's (common) sense. It's natural enough. Look at sports. I played basketball on the playgrounds of Charlotte, North Carolina, for a long time. In fact, I was something of a legend (in my own mind, of course) at Park Road Park. You know how I did it? I examined how teams lose and then determined how not to do that. But more was required, not just playing *not to lose*, but learning how to and playing—*to win*! How did Adam figure it out?

Adam did not continue to hide. Once God found him and Eve, they both stayed to hear what God had to say. Unlike most people today, as disobedient and ashamed as Adam was, he stood before God and *listened* to Him. Adam not only listened to God, but he *believed* Him.

God told the serpent (that had Satan in it):

> **And I will cause hostility between you and the woman,**
> **and between your offspring and her offspring. He will**
> **strike your head, and you will strike his heel.**
>
> – Genesis 3:15 (NLT)

Adam believed God when The Father told Satan there would be one who would fix this situation of disobedience. One would be born of "the woman" who would "strike his head" (destroy the Devil) while Satan would only "strike his heel" (wound the child). Now I know this doesn't translate well, so let me give you a clear picture of Adam's belief.

> **Now the man called his wife's name Eve, because she was**
> **the mother of all the living.**
>
> – Genesis 3:20 (NASB)

Adam gave his wife her name, "Eve," which meant "the mother of all who live." Why would he name her that? Perhaps he knew her destiny? Perhaps God gave Adam a little peek behind the curtain? Regardless, Adam knew Eve was to be the mother of all who came after her.

Adam was a man who possessed hope of life beyond his and his wife's disobedience. God said Adam would have offspring, and because he had none at that time, he would have to be alive long enough to have at least one. Here Adam turns away from Satan and stops trusting or obeying his lies. Instead he turns to the truth about God and trusts His word. That's called repentance.

repent re·pent \ri-ˈpent: to feel or show that you are sorry for something bad or wrong that you did
and that you want to do what is right

– Merriam-Webster Dictionary

"So we could put it this way: the attitude of Adam was dramatically changed toward God and toward Satan. No longer would he believe the liar, who brought this evil upon him; he would believe God. Once a believer only in God, he had defected to become a believer in the serpent, a follower of God's enemy--the lying Devil--but in the very words of naming Eve, Adam demonstrates that he believes God's word and is anticipating its fulfillment, including the destruction of Satan, his former master."

– John MacArthur, American pastor, author, teacher

Do you think Adam would have stood in front of God and listened and trusted what God had to say, especially because he was still alive, if he had not "repented"? Think he might have been just *this* side of overjoyed (done his happy dance, in fact) that God had not struck him dead on the spot? Not only that, but don't you think Adam was relieved that his offspring was going to pay Satan back for deceiving his wife and initiating the breakdown of their relationship with God? No, I think Adam was glad to be given the opportunity to do the right thing—again. He had *faith* in God. And in this gesture, God showed His *grace*.

Not only did God *not* kill Adam and Eve on the spot (mercy) but he allowed them to be the gateway from which one would come to reconcile this whole relationship between God and Man forever (grace). God didn't have to do either. He was under no obligation. He gave both mercy and grace freely, not only by not killing Adam physically (although the pure relationship with God would be crippled) but also instilling Adam with faith to believe God.

Yes, God was *hot*. Man was disobedient. But Man *did* say he was sorry; even further, Man believed in God again. There's one little point I want to make here, before we go on, but will harp on a lot more later in the book. GOD PUT THE FAITH IN ADAM TO BELIEVE AGAIN! (Ephesians 2:8-9). God Himself reconciled the whole situation.

Good to be Home.

> *"Reunited, and it feels so good. Reunited 'cause we understood. There's one perfect fit and, sugar, this one is it. We both are so excited 'cause we're reunited."*
>
> – Peaches and Herb, *Reunited*

> *God was in Christ reconciling the world to Himself, not counting their trespasses against them.*
>
> – 2 Corinthians 5:19 (NASB)

Have you ever been on a long trip? You know, away from home for an extended period of time? When I was in the Navy, I was gone from the U.S. for three months. It seemed like an eternity. While I was gone, I got a *Dear John* letter from my girlfriend. Bummer. Now I know this is the part where I'm supposed to tell you that when I got home, we got back together and everything was cool.

Well—she married some other guy, and they had their honeymoon in Paris. I know, I know. It's not exactly the relevant, feel-good story for our topic of reconciliation. Except, it gives me a very small taste of what God *could have* done to Man. ***Grace abounds*** (Romans 5:20).

God took pity on Adam and Eve's shame and guilt about their nakedness. As earlier stated, their shame was a result of the guilt they felt from their disobedience. This guilt caused them to be separated from God and to lose the spiritual relationship. But God still loved them. To show His love, He wanted to repair their relationship. God wanted Man reconciled unto Him. Because Man couldn't do anything about the situation, God did. He sacrificed an animal in the garden to cover their nakedness, their guilt.

This animal wasn't guilty of anything. It was used just to cover the nakedness, the sin of Man. In this way, God showed Man that a sacrificial death was necessary to cover sin. The idea that an innocent life must be offered to cover sins began right there.

While this animal served the purpose of covering Man's sin, it was an imperfect Band-Aid™ for the relationship that had been so severely damaged by Adam's disobedience. For thousands of years, from Adam to Abel to Noah and all who came after, innocent animals had to be slaughtered and accepted as covering of Man's sin. But Man used the covering as an excuse to sin.

See, the problem with animal sacrifices is that they are only a symbol. Because God can't immediately kill the people who sinned, the same ones with whom He wanted to have a relationship (else there would be no people), an animal had to die to "cover" or take the place for a human's sin. The only problem with that was the people used the animals, not as a *symbol* of their dying to sin, but as a *substitute* for obedience.

It was a get-out-of-jail-free card. "Heh, I sinned, so let's find an animal to kill. I can go right on being disobedient, as long as I can kill another animal. I sin, I kill, I sin, I kill… Life is good." However, God got a *little* fed up with that.

> *What makes you think I want all your sacrifices?" says the*
> *Lord. "I am sick of your burnt offerings of rams and the*
> *fat of fattened cattle. I get no pleasure from the blood*
> *of bulls and lambs and goats. When you come to worship*
> *me, who asked you to parade through my courts with*
> *all your ceremony? When you lift up your hands in prayer,*
> *I will not look. Though you offer many prayers….*
> *Wash yourselves and be clean! Get your sins out of my*
> *sight. Give up your evil ways."*
>
> – Isaiah 1:11-16 (NLT)

God wanted a permanent solution, a solution Man couldn't mess up (*'cause if Man can, Man will*). Man needed a better sin covering. Instead of creating a symbol of sacrifice that didn't mean anything to the sinner, God wanted a real change of heart. So He decided to change Man's heart Himself.

> *I'm going to give you a new heart, and I'm going to give*
> *you a new spirit within all of your deepest parts. I'll remove*
> *that rock-hard heart of yours and replace it with one that's*
> *sensitive to me.*
>
> – Ezekiel 36:26 (ISV)

God performed a little spiritual surgery. He devised a way to replace that unrepentant, prideful, selfish heart (Man's feeling, will and intellect) and dead spirit with a new heart and a living spirit that is willing and able to obey God. This replacement heart and spirit would be so good that it would allow God to again have a right relationship with Man. God could then look on Man as if he had never sinned at all! He could *reconcile* Himself to Man.

However, in keeping with his standard of death to cover sin, a sacrifice would need to be given. But not just any sacrifice. This sacrifice would need to take away the sin of the world. What sacrifice could be that perfect and far-reaching? The only sacrifice that would do would be …Himself! Stay with me here.

You remember Adam's offspring, the one who would crush the serpent's head? You might have heard of Him. His name is Jesus. Jesus came to Earth, God as Man, both fully Man and fully God.

Want to know how God pulled that off? Well, we could go into a discussion of the Trinity (God the Father, God the Son, and God the Holy Spirit, or God in three persons); however, because some of the greatest theologians (studiers of God) have written books on that subject, suffice it to say—He did it.

Only God the Son, Jesus, could pay the full cost of Man's disobedience to God the Father. Jesus was perfect as Man, so He had no sin for which to be punished. And as God, he would be big enough and eternal; sufficient to carry the punishment, or the wrath of God against the sinner, for all time. Let me paraphrase a story I read on the *Word of Hope Ministries* Web site (*http://www.jesus-islam.org/Pages/TheVickinking.aspx*) that might enlighten the concept.

There was a king who heard someone was stealing in the village. The king said that whoever was caught for these thefts would be given 100 lashes with the whip. That would have been a death penalty, for no one had ever survived 100 lashes.

After a while, the thief was caught. Lo and behold, it was the king's mother!! The villagers buzzed with anticipation. What would the king do? Would he go back on his word and not dispense justice and seem a weak and fickle king? Or would he dispense justice at the cost of his mother and be an uncaring and hard ruler? (I gotta believe this is where Reality TV started.)

When his mother came before the king, the villagers were deathly silent as the charges were read, the verdict presented, and the sentence given. Thievery, guilty, 100 lashes. So the king had kept his word, and justice prevailed. But then something amazing happened.

As his mother was tied to the stake and her back exposed, the king came down from his throne, took off his royal robe, exposed his own back, covered his mother, and said to the executioner … "BEGIN." And the king was whipped until he died.

That's what God did for Man. He reconciled Himself unto Himself. God the Father used God the Son (who was every bit God) to reconcile Himself to Man. It was the only way. Through the sacrifice of Jesus on the cross, through his suffering and death, God's justice was served. The sacrificial death required to pay the cost of sin (that result being Man's physical and spiritual death) was provided. Once and for all, no more sacrifices would be required to prevent our spiritual deaths. The cost was paid. God's perfect plan is fulfilled.

Jesus sacrificed as a man for all Men; anyone who believes that He did and acts accordingly will be reconciled to God.

> *…that if you confess with your mouth Jesus as Lord, and believe in your heart that God raised Him from the dead, you will be saved….*
>
> – Romans 10:9-10

Jesus, through his sacrifice, allows God to be the God of justice and mercy and grace. For if you believe that Jesus is God who came to Earth as Man to pay the cost for your disobedience, then you will be reconciled to God.

That's right, you now have available a Savior; the One who has saved you from the power and penalty of sin. The power of sin causes us to believe we can disobey God. The penalty of sin is to be forever without God (Hell). You can have a right relationship with the God of the Universe if you want it.

THE TRUE BENEFIT OF JESUS AS SAVIOR IS FOUND IN RECONCILIATION TO GOD.

The Value of Christ as Savior - Part 1: The Benefits

Having sufficient information on Jesus Christ as Savior, let's turn the info into knowledge. Let's use it. This transformation from information to knowledge is based on using what we've previously gathered. To determine the value of Christ as Savior, we subtract the cost from the benefit. So—here we go.

We ended last time with the proclamation:

THE TRUE BENEFIT OF JESUS AS SAVIOR IS FOUND IN RECONCILIATION TO GOD.

Perhaps in my enthusiasm I jumped the gun a little. I should have saved that for this chapter (but I got a bit excited and wanted to have a big finish and…well, you know how it is). Anyway, the natural question that comes from such a proclamation is: *So what? What's the big deal with being reconciled to God?*

Are we going to return to Eden? Do women stop having birth pains? Do men stop becoming frustrated with their work? Does the world stop its decay? Do we turn back the clock to the time when we (and the world) were perfect? Ahhh…no. That train, the perfection-on-Earth train, has left the station. It will take a "new Earth" for that to happen. Suffice it to say that the benefit of the Savior is two-fold: what we are saved from and what we are saved to.

"Saved from…."

"When the Fox hears the Rabbit scream he comes a-runnin', but not to help."
– Hannibal Lector, *Silence of the Lambs* (1991)

"I have told you these things so that in Me you may have peace. You will have suffering in this world. Be courageous! I have conquered the world."

– John 16:33

Saved from what? We've discussed what separation from God means both in terms of physical and spiritual death. With Jesus Christ as Savior, we are "saved" from death (Matthew 1:21).

Jesus came to Earth to save his people from their sins, to seek and to save those who were lost. Could it be *lost* in the sense that we do not know that we need to have a right relationship with God? Or perhaps lost in the sense that without this right relationship with God we will suffer forever in the pit of Hell?

Both are true; however, Jesus is seeking, looking for those people who know they are lost (Luke 19:10). They know there's something wrong: wrong with the world, wrong with their lives, just plain wrong. And they can't fix it. But while just about everyone will agree that the world is broken, few will admit that the most broken part of it is—*wait for it*—themselves! There's a reason for that.

As with Adam and Eve, there is something inherently evil in every Man. It started with The Fall and has increased ever since. The same entity that aids in the increase awoke sin in Man: Satan. He uses the world to make what is wrong appear right, and what is evil appear good. He creates a Satanic standard, one that tickles the itchy ear of a sin-sick population (2 Timothy 4:3).

God gave Man a conscience to distinguish wrong from right (Romans 2:13-15). But just as Satan deceived Eve, he continues to deceive Man. By creating an environment where God's word and truth are replaced with Man-centered pride and selfishness, Satan has taken Man's conscience and twisted it from something that points to God to something that points to Man.

When life is a struggle and you're realizing that you're lost, what does Satan do? Oh, he comes a runnin' with "Life Takes Visa." If you just had more money, more fame, more status, a shrink, (or a better *Dr.-Everything'll-Be-All-Right*), or more of whatever else he can throw your way to convince you that "Yes, you're lost, but here's how to be found! Here's how to clear up the fog in your life!" I can give you a quick understanding of the concept.

I was in jail back in July 2008. Having nothing available to kill time but a Gideon's Bible, I started to read, coming upon this section of the Book of Romans:

> **I want to do what is right, but I can't. I want to do what**
> **is good, but I don't. I don't want to do what is wrong,**
> **but I do it anyway.**
>
> – Romans 7:18-19 (NLT)

See, I knew there was a right and wrong. My momma taught me that. But God put it in me first, just like He did in every person. Don't you have to justify what you do? How do you do that? Don't you use a *standard* of what is right and wrong to *determine* what is right and wrong?

For much of the western European world, that standard is called the Judeo-Christian ethic (external standard). In America, whether we'd like to admit it or not (and this country is swiftly approaching "or not" point), we get our ethics from the Bible.

With these ethics come our morals (internal standard). When a situation comes up, we use ethics to determine morals. We use the concepts of the Bible (sometimes) to determine what we should do.

Well, that standard, as twisted and perverted as Man has allowed it to become (from the perfected standard Adam and Eve initially lived), is established in God's standard. God is The Determiner of right and wrong. And there is still a very, very, very small sliver of that standard left in Man. OK, back to the story.

So there I was in jail, with the truth of my life staring at me from the pages of this book. That was me, wanting to do "right" (like my conscience and my momma said) but not being able to. Something was wrong. I was broken. If I want to do right but can't, something is amiss. How do I fix it? Well, I tried to fix it; that's what landed me in jail. "If you just had more money, you could buy more crack, chase more women, and basically fix that hole in your soul." How'd that standard work out for me? Well—it sounded like a good idea at the time.

So sitting in my jail cell, I read:

> *For the mind that is set on the flesh is hostile to God, for it does not submit to God's law; indeed, it cannot. Those who are in the flesh cannot please God. You, however are not in the flesh but in the Spirit, if in fact the Spirit of God dwells in you.*
>
> – Roman 8:7-9

Hey…I DON'T FIX IT: I CAN'T FIX IT! THE WORLD CAN'T FIX IT!!! It's spiritual, not Earthly. There has to be some other way to fix it. He is called the Spirit. The Holy Spirit is the One who will "fix" me. Now I could tell you how the jail cell literally lit up with this revelation, but you probably wouldn't believe me anyway, so I won't.

The bottom line is that this whole scenario works only if you know that you're broken and need fixing. And you have to stop wanting to be broken. You have to want to be fixed. No longer *wanting* to be broken and wanting to be fixed is the same as wanting to turn away from your disobedience to God and turn to obedience to God. That's called repentance. You want to repent. But what does all this have to do with Jesus Christ as Savior?

Give It Your Best Try.

> *"Do or do not. There is no try."*
>
> – Yoda, *Star Wars: Episode V – The Empire Strikes Back* (1980)

> *We are all like one who is unclean, all our so-called*
> *righteous acts are like a menstrual rag in your sight. We*
> *all wither like a leaf; our sins carry us away like the wind.*
>
> – Isaiah 64:6 (NET)

I've made progress, recognized that I am lost and that I need some way to get on the right road. I'll try to do right. Oh, I tried that already. Okay, I'll go to church...oh, tried that already. What about prayer? Check. Result: zippo. What is the problem? The problem was that I was trying to get on the right road, only I was stuck in a ditch. I needed a tow truck.

Sinners are dead (Ephesians 2:1). You remember we talked about spiritual death with Adam and Eve? Well, that's the natural state of Man, dead to the ways of God. Yeah, you have a conscience, but that tells you about only the law of God, not God Himself. It shows you what Man needs to do to keep from blowing the world into oblivion (that's God's job (2 Peter 3:10)). Your conscience is not the perfect righteousness of God.

God requires perfection, remember? And let's face it, when was the last time someone (lied and) told you that you were perfect? So all your efforts at trying to find God are useless. Good works? A soiled Kotex™ is cleaner. Prayer? Save your breath; He doesn't hear you (John 9:31). Sacrificing for Him? Good luck with that (Psalm 51:16). Think you're doing good for God? Don't bet on it (Matthew 7:23-24). **Only** by the Holy Spirit are we saved.

> *He saved us, not on the basis of deeds which we have*
> *done in righteousness, but according to His mercy,*
> *by the washing of regeneration and renewing by the*
> *Holy Spirit.*
>
> – Titus 3:5 (NASB)

The Holy Spirit of God comes into you only if you have faith in the power of Jesus to reconcile you with God (John 16:7). So if Jesus did not "go away" (die on the cross and come back to life on the third day), then the Helper (the Holy Spirit) would not have come.

- If you don't believe in what Christ can do, you can't have the Holy Spirit.

- If the Holy Spirit is not enlightening you, you won't understand the truth.

- If you can't become enlightened to the truth, you can't be saved from the power and penalty of your sin.

- In short, without repentance and believing in Jesus as Savior, you can't be saved.

But, again, saved from what? You can be saved from the power and penalty of sin. Although we've discussed this concept before, I'd like to take a few paragraphs to expand upon it.

The Power is Super.

Superman: "I've got you."
Lois Lane: "You've got me? Who's got you?"

– Superman (1978)

The Spirit of God, who raised Jesus from the dead, lives in you. And just as God raised Christ Jesus from the dead, he will give life to your mortal bodies by this same Spirit living within you.

– Romans 8:11 (NLT)

The power of sin is that which makes you disobedient (Are you noticing a theme here?). Sin is the power that causes you to give in to your lustful desires to do what you want to do and not what God wants you to do. (James 1:14).

This want to do your own thing is based on your pride and selfishness. Admitting that you're prideful and selfish would be nice, but one of the sneaky things about pride and selfishness is that they appear to you as the "right thing for you." *Why is it wrong to get what is right for me?* That sounds perfectly OK, right? Only it's not. Because *God* decides what is right and right for you.

Before Adam and Eve disobeyed and ate the fruit, they understood and agreed that God knew what was right for them. Know why? Because they obeyed Him! Would you obey a command that you didn't think would be good for you? No way. You have to see something of benefit to you. Only our pride and selfishness refuse to let God decide what is good for us. You say to yourself, "I got this."

But Jesus saves us from this mindset. Through the power of the Holy Spirit, who comes after you acknowledge faith in Christ, you have the power to resist that urge to be disobedient. The urge to sin is still there, but now you have something you didn't have before. You have a *choice* to sin or not. Before Christ came into your heart, you didn't even know what the truly perfect, Godly good was!

So you are saved from the power of sin. But you also are saved from the penalty of sin. Because we have all sinned and fallen short of God's standard, we all are judged guilty and sentenced to the penalty our sin deserves. That penalty is death, first the physical death and then the spiritual death.

> *And just as it is appointed for man to die once, and after that comes judgment, so Christ, having been offered once to bear the sins of many.*
>
> – Hebrews 9:27

Jesus "did the time for your crime." He paid the penalty for your sin. Your eternity in Hell is gone. Complete separation from what is peaceful and joyful and ...God, won't happen. Jesus saves us from what we deserve as disobedient creations of the Great Creator. Jesus saves.

But He not only saves us *from* the power and penalty of sin. He saves us *to* the reward of being reconciled to God. Now we should better understand the benefits of Jesus as Savior, having turned the information we've previously received into knowledge. We understand the benefit; now let's consider the cost.

The Value of Christ as Savior –
Part 2: The Cost

That is why I said that you will die in your sins; for unless
you believe that I Am who I claim to be, you will die in
your sins.

– John 8:24 (NLT)

Now that I am a Believer (in Jesus Christ), it seems such a natural thing to believe what the Bible states. Perhaps I believed it and just didn't do anything with that belief. And that is a part of the cost of Jesus as Savior. You must believe. This belief comes in three forms: knowledge, emotion, and will.

For this people's heart has grown dull, and with their
ears they can barely hear, and their eyes they have
closed, lest they should see with their eyes and hear
with their ears and understand with their heart and
turn, and I would heal them.

– Matthew 13:15 (ESV)

Let's start with the eyes and ears, then discuss the heart.

Peek-a-Boo, I See You.

"We can run, but we can't hide from it. Of all possible worlds,
we only got one: we gotta to ride on it.
Whatever we've done, we'll never get far from what we
leave behind...."

– The Grateful Dead, *We Can Run, But We Can't Hide*

> *"Now hear this, O foolish and senseless people, Who have*
> *eyes but do not see; Who have ears but do not hear."*
>
> – Jeremiah 5:21 (NASB)

The cost of Christ as Savior starts with hearing and receiving the Word of God. You have to be willing to listen and perceive. Remember how we discussed that Adam hid from God in the Garden, yet when God spoke, Adam listened? That's you. You can run and hide from God all you want, but you can't escape Him (Psalm 139:7). No matter where you go, there He is.

> *"We cannot see God, but he can see us. The psalmist did not*
> *desire to go from the Lord. Whither can I go? In the most*
> *distant corners of the world, in heaven, or in hell, I cannot go*
> *out of thy reach. No veil can hide us from God; not the thickest*
> *darkness. No disguise can save any person or action from being*
> *seen in the true light by him."*
>
> – Matthew Henry, British minister and author

So God is talking to you constantly. No, not audibly. There's no booming voice from the heavens; no whisper in your ear; no e-mail, text, or tweet saying, "Hey, it's God. Repent and Believe!!" Granted, you might find your way into a sermon, or a testimony from a mouthpiece of God, a Believer. But are you going to take the time to hear it? More importantly, are you going to take the time to listen? You hear with your ears, you listen with your mind.

And you see God all around you (Romans 1:20). You call it luck or chance or coincidence. Dude, that's God. When you do something you know is wrong and you get away with it, that's God's mercy not striking you dead right then and there. When you get something good that you know you didn't deserve, that's God's grace. Every day and in every way you see God at work in your life.

Even when you grumble and complain that you're jobless or homeless or in prison or in any other apparently Godless situation, God is right there. God is there, you just don't acknowledge Him.

Yes, they knew God, but they wouldn't worship him as
God or even give him thanks. And they began to think up
foolish ideas of what God was like. As a result, their
minds became dark and confused.

– Romans 1:21 (NLT)

Don't you see how wonderfully kind, tolerant, and patient
God is with you? Does this mean nothing to you? Can't you
see that his kindness is intended to turn you from your sin?
But because you are stubborn and refuse to turn from your
sin, you are storing up terrible punishment for yourself. For
a day of anger is coming, when God's righteous judgment
will be revealed.

– Romans 2:4-5 (NLT)

I tell guys in prison that the best thing that ever happened to me was going to jail. (Some people must think, "Wow, your life must have been really bad.") I say that because in jail I wasn't distracted by this world: the lust of the flesh, the lust of the eyes, and the pride of life. Jail didn't cloud my vision or dull my hearing. It allowed both to become more clear. Without the distractions I could pay attention to God.

Are you so prideful that even *God* can't tell you anything? You listen, right up until the time the call to Christ interferes *wit yo' flow*. Don't act like you don't know what I'm talking about. There are Believers with neither eye looking to Heaven and both eyes fixed on Earth. So if *saved* folk don't want their Earthly *saved* lives interrupted, imagine how some of those corrupted heathens (of which I was once one (1 Corinthians 16:11)) could do without heavenly intervention?

God called stubborn people "stiff-necked." They act like a horse with a bit in its mouth that doesn't want to turn his neck when the rider pulls the reins. They're stiff-necked. They're willful and their will is not to go in the direction of the guy with reigns, but to go their own way.

"Stiff-necked fools, you think you are cool
To deny me for simplicity
Yes, you have gone for so long
With your love for vanity, now
Yes, you have got the wrong interpretation
Mixed up with vain imagination."
– Bob Marley & The Wailers, *Stiff-Necked Fools*

The cost of Christ is to give up your deaf ear and blind eye and accept the knowledge provided about who Christ is and what He came to do as truth. After you hear and see God's truth comes your emotion, which is working on that hard heart.

The Shape of My Heart.

"I know that the spades are the swords of a soldier
I know that the clubs are weapons of war
I know that diamonds mean money for this art
But that's not the shape of my heart."
– Sting, *Shape of My Heart*

And I will give you a new heart, and I will put a new spirit
in you. I will take out your stony, stubborn heart and give
you a tender, responsive heart.
– Ezekiel 36:26 (NLT)

Jesus Christ as your Savior will cost you a "hard" heart. Although the Hebrew understanding of heart includes the three components of intellect, emotion, and will, for this particular discussion, we use heart for the emotional part of the trilogy.

(In other parts of the book we might discuss the heart differently, and if so, we'll let you know.)

> ***The sacrifice pleasing to God is a broken spirit. God,***
> ***You will not despise a broken and humbled heart.***
>
> – Psalm 51:17 (HCSB)

God wants you to give up your hard-heartedness. After hearing about the sacrifice Christ made for you and me, that he didn't wait until we "got ourselves together" or "stopped sinning," but instead died for you while you were deep in your sin, you should have a broken heart! You should be so very, very sorrowful for having messed up so bad that Jesus had to die for you. He did the same for my filthy excuse of a life!

Would you do the same for those who spat in your face (For me it's on right there! Forgive me. I'm still a work in progress.), slapped you and beat you with their fists, flogged you with a metal-tipped whip, nailed your hands and feet to a cross, and then drove a spear through your side? Would you die for that person? The people who did all those things, those people, are you and me.

> ***When we were utterly helpless, Christ came at just the right***
> ***time and died for us sinners. Now, most people would not***
> ***be willing to die for an upright person, though someone***
> ***might perhaps be willing to die for a person who is***
> ***especially good. But God showed his great love for us by***
> ***sending Christ to die for us while we were still sinners.***
>
> – Romans 5:6-8 (NLT)

Every time you reject the call, every time you put yourself ahead of Christ, every time you choose to be disobedient instead of repenting of your sins, you strike another blow into the nails, rip another path through His back, deliver another slap, another fist, more spit. IT WAS, AND IS, YOU!!

Have you no compassion for Him who died for you? Soften your heart, feel His love for you. But you ask yourself, "What has this to do with me? It was the Jews who killed Christ, or the Romans or history or God or…or…me?" Christ was crucified for your sin (Isaiah 53:5).

> *"What shall I render to the Lord for all of his benefits to me?"*
> *the reply was, "I will lift the cup of salvation and call upon the*
> *name of the Lord" (Psalm 116:12-13). So, translating that …*
> *Jesus gives us the gift of himself and we ask, "Now what can I*
> *render to Jesus for all the benefits of his fellowship?" Answer:*
> *Ask him for his help. That's the gift he wants."*
>
> – John Piper, American theologian, pastor, and author

If you can ask for His help, and mean that, then you will receive a new heart. Your old heart would never mean it. So with acknowledgement and repentance comes faith. And faith is based on will. You have to give up your will. The cost of Christ as Savior is your will.

> *Father, if you are willing, please take this cup of suffering*
> *away from me. Yet I want your will to be done, not mine.*
>
> – Luke 22:42 (NLT)

Those were the words of Jesus Christ hours before He went to the cross. The suffering He spoke of was not the physical, but the spiritual. God the Son had never known separation from God the Father. Ever. Before ever. Before time. Let's put it like this: there was no time in all of the infinity that preceded the crucifixion that God the Son did not have perfect unity with God the Father. (I know I can't understand that either; it's too deep for me.)

Yet Christ was willing to do the will of His Father. *"Not my will, but yours."* That is the cost of salvation. The cost of Christ as Savior is doing what *God* wants you to do over what *you* want to do. What does God want you to do?

I Believe in Miracles.

> *"I believe... I believe... It's silly, but I believe."*
> — Susan, *Miracle on 34th Street*

> ***Repent of your sins and believe the Good News!***
> — Mark 1:15

Believe. Believe what?

- That I am disobedient to God and through that disobedience I am an enemy of God. (Romans 5:10, James 4:4)

- That there is no other way to be reconciled to God except through the sacrifice of Jesus Christ. (Acts 4:11-12)

- That Jesus is all God. (John 1:1, 1:14, 8:58, 10:30)

- That Jesus is all Man. (John 20:27, Acts 2:22-23, 1 Timothy 2:5, Romans 5:15)

- That as a perfect Man He can take the penalty of death that comes from my disobedience. (1 John 2:2)

- That God thought Christ was perfect and raised Him from the dead because He never disobeyed.

- And that through my belief in all this, I will obey God. (Jeremiah 31:33)

Believe all this? Well—yes. Yeah, I know, that's quite a list. There is one passage that sums up all this stuff.

> *... that if you confess with your mouth Jesus as Lord, and*
> *believe in your heart that God raised Him from the dead,*
> *you will be saved; for with the heart a person believes,*
> *resulting in righteousness, and with the mouth he*
> *confesses, resulting in salvation.*
>
> – Romans 10:9-10 (NASB)

Can you give up your will, your desires, your wants, your dreams, and your life for God? Jesus demands that. Follow Jesus, the Son of God. Walk as He walked, talk as He talked, suffer as He suffered, and die, if necessary, as He died. Give up your will for His. If He makes you a millionaire, fine. If He makes you homeless and penniless, fine. If you live to be a hundred, fine. If you die tomorrow, fine. Your will is His will, because your life is now committed to His command (Galatians 2:20).

The cost of Christ as Savior is your knowledge, your emotion, and your will. The cost will be your *life* as you currently know it.

The Value of Christ as Savior – Part 3: The Equation

"Today I have given you the choice between life and death, between blessings and curses. Now I call on heaven and Earth to witness the choice you make. Oh, that you would choose life, so that you and your descendants might live."

– Deuteronomy 30:19 (NLT)

I will not labor you with further talk on the benefit and cost of Christ as Savior. It is a fairly simple decision: blessing or cursing, Heaven or Hell, obedience or disobedience, trust in God or trust in Self.

We've gathered data, turned it into information, and then into knowledge. It's time for a little application of knowledge, wisdom. This is the right time to review our Value Equation.Like the simple decision above, the Value Equation is equally as simple:

The Value of Christ as Savior = Benefit – Cost

or

Value of Christ as Savior =

What You Are Saved From – Control of Your Life

See how easy this is? Now, choose. What's the problem? Hasn't the argument for and against, benefit and cost, pro and con been made? Go ahead, choose! Isn't this the same way the local church talks to you when they give the altar call? "Come on down!! What's the hold-up?"

Although tomorrow is not promised, and we'd rather you came to Christ now rather than take the chance that a plane falls on you while you're reading this, we'd like you to make a wise and thoughtful decision. At least, that's what the Bible states:

> *If you want to be my disciple, you must hate everyone else by comparison—your father and mother, wife and children, brothers and sisters—yes, even your own life. Otherwise, you cannot be my disciple. And if you do not carry your own cross and follow me, you cannot be my disciple. "But don't begin until you count the cost. (emphasis added) For who would begin construction of a building without first calculating the cost to see if there is enough money to finish it? Otherwise, you might complete only the foundation before running out of money, and then everyone would laugh at you. They would say, 'There's the person who started that building and couldn't afford to finish it!'*
>
> – Luke 14:26-30 (NLT)

Do not fool yourself. Giving up your will for the will of God is not easy. In fact, it's impossible without the Holy Spirit (and it's no hayride even with Him). Following Christ is a difficult journey, once you commit. But God will supply whatever you need for His glory and your good.

We are not ones to advocate hasty decisions. Oh no, there is more data to collect, more information to be determined and more knowledge and wisdom to be found and used. For there is no point in discussing Jesus as Savior if we do not continue the discussion with Jesus as Lord.

By now you readers should be spiritual rocket scientists, so we won't format the three-step process as before. We'll combine the data, information and knowledge concepts to provide you with a more even flow of thought behind the benefit and cost of Jesus Christ.

Our hope is that in this way you can develop a pattern of thought that quickly progresses you from where you are to where you need to be in order to form an accurate and beneficial decision. Okay? *Heeeeeeeeere* we go….!

Jesus Christ as Lord

Introduction

lord \'lȯrd\: one having power and authority over others

– Merriam-Webster Dictionary

When Believers speak of Jesus Christ as Lord, this is what we mean: Jesus has power and authority over our lives. When we repented of our sins, asked to be saved from the power, penalty, and presence of sin, and asked to be made right with God, we also asked Jesus to become our Lord.

> *And the jailer called for lights and rushed in, and*
> *trembling with fear he fell down before Paul and Silas.*
> *Then he brought them out and said, "Sirs, what must*
> *I do to be saved?" And they said, "Believe in the Lord*
> *Jesus, and you will be saved…."*

– Acts 16:29-31(ESV)

Well, that should be clear. *Believe and you're saved.* The issue is, believe... WHAT? When the Scripture says believe in the Lord Jesus, what does that mean? Believe that He existed? Believe that He was a good man, a prophet, a humanitarian, the CEO of a non-profit? No, believe that Jesus is Savior and Lord. Romans 10:9-10 explains the two-pronged Earthly salvation. First, **believe in your heart that God raised Him from the dead.**

But Believe means more than acknowledgement; Believing means that something matters to you, that you care. After all:

> *You believe that there is one God. Good! Even the demons*
> *believe that—and shudder.*

– James 2:19

One must accept that all this believing leads to something they want, namely salvation.

So Believe means that you acknowledge: (1) Jesus was sinless, and therefore could die for your sins, (2) Jesus was God, infinitely sinless enough to die for the sins of all who want to be saved, (3) God the Father acknowledged both of these facts by raising Jesus from the grave, and (4) That this is sufficient for you to be justified before God.

However, the concept of Jesus as Savior is relevant only if Jesus is Lord. Now this revelation might come as a shock to many, even those who confess Jesus as Savior. Confess with your mouth that Jesus Christ is Lord, that you accept and come under the power and authority of Jesus over your life.

Here's where it gets interesting. Jesus is Lord whether you believe He is or not. In fact, He's Lord of Believers and non-Believers. Hold on, don't get confused. The Bible clearly states:

> *... so that at the name of Jesus EVERY KNEE WILL*
> *BOW, of those who are in Heaven and on Earth and*
> *under the Earth, and that every tongue will confess*
> *that Jesus Christ is Lord, to the glory of God the Father.*
> – Philippians 2:10-11(NASB)

You see folks, He might not be everybody's Savior, but He is everybody's Lord. The fact that some do not confess Him as Savior, well that's on them. But in the end, EVERYONE will confess that Jesus Christ is Lord—of all. How can we say that? Jesus said it Himself:

> *And Jesus came up and spoke to them, saying, "All*
> *authority has been given to Me in Heaven and on Earth."*
> – Matthew 28:18 (NASB)

And Paul restates it:

And he put all things under his feet and gave him as
head over all things to the church.

– Ephesians 1:22 (ESV)

Upon Jesus's return from the grave, God the Father gave God the Son all authority over all things. And while there are some places in the Bible where all, in context, does not mean every (Mark 1:5, John 8:2, Matthew 10:22, John 3:26, to list a few)—this ain't one of them! In this case, all means every single one.

Christ has authority over everything. The living and the dead, Heaven and Hell, and…stay with me…Believers and non-Believers! Just because you don't believe it, like it, or follow it, doesn't make it any less true. In fact, when Christ returns, you'll see what I mean.

So it's not a question of whether Christ is Lord, but rather, whether you *acknowledge* Him as Lord over your life. Because eventually, all will acknowledge that He is Lord over their lives. Only for those of you who didn't acknowledge it on Earth, while you're still breathing, His authority will damn you to Hell.

For the Father judges no one, but has given all judgment to the Son.

– John 5:22 (ESV)

Jesus was Lord in the Old Testament. Jesus was Lord in the New Testament. Jesus is Lord then, now, and forever.

"... for that he does judge is certain; he is the Judge of the whole Earth; he is God that judgeth in the Earth, or governs the world with his Son, who works together in the affairs of providence: he judged and condemned the old world, but not without his Son, who by his Spirit, or in his divine nature, went and preached to the spirits now in prison, then disobedient in the times of Noah; he judged and condemned Sodom and Gomorrah, but not without the Son; for Jehovah the Son rained, from Jehovah the Father, fire and brimstone upon those cities, and consumed them; he judged the people of Israel, and often chastised them for their sins, but not without his Son angel of his presence that went before them; he judges all men, and justifies and acquits whom he pleases, but not without his Son."

– Gill's Exposition of the Whole Bible

That's it in a nutshell. He's your Lord; obey and go to Heaven. He's your Lord; disobey and go to Hell. Simple enough? Good, let's continue. The value of Christ as Lord is based on a destination, a conclusion, a point in time. If I am saved, I am saved not only *from* something but *to* something.

Let me show you an example of this: drug rehab. I went to a few classes, and you know what I noticed? People were drinking 700 cups of coffee, smoking a pack of cigarettes during the break, and scarfing down as many doughnuts and cookies as time would allow. Yeah, they might not have been using their drug of choice, but they were replacing that drug with caffeine, nicotine, and sugar. But, hey, they weren't doing *illegal* drugs, so life is good, right?

My point is that if you leave one place, you end up somewhere else. No matter where you go, there you are. If you accept the benefit of Jesus as Savior and leave the path to Hell, you are currently—where? This concept of coming from somewhere and going to somewhere is the basic concept of repentance.

"Two requisites of repentance ... "to turn from evil, and to turn to the good."
                                                                    – Bible Study Tools

This concept of repentance, though lost on the majority of Christians today, is vital to obtaining the full benefit of Christ as Lord. After all, if you just want to go to Heaven, wouldn't Jesus dying for your sins and reconciling you to God the Father be sufficient? *Can't He just save me and let me party like it's 1999?* Uh— no. Remember the two-pronged salvation on Earth?

To confess Jesus as Lord is the second prong; that's call *sanctification.* People, Christians weren't saved, or justified (the first prong), to be in right standing with God so they could do whatever they please. Who exactly do they think they are?

Yet a loud group of *Christians* (and I use that term in categorical, not spiritual terms) believe you can be saved from something now, but you can wait to be saved to something later. (You might or might not have heard of them, the NO-LORDSHIP-SALVATION crowd.) That is, you are justified (in right standing with God, having accepted Christ is your Savior) immediately upon believing in Christ, yet you don't immediately need to accept that Christ is your Lord. Well— if we stay true to "no matter where you go, there you are," then where are you after you become justified? I turn from evil to...?

"Oh I'm so happy I'm not going to Hell, that I'm in right standing with God, that I'll just keep on doing what I was doing before I was in right standing with God." Kinda begs the question: *If God didn't want you to do something different, why did He save you in the first place?* What? What's that you say? "Why not? I'm not that bad of a person. I do good stuff!" Really? You do remember from Romans 3:10-12 that God considers not one of us here on Earth good without Him? Salvation is about being saved from something to something.

> ***For those whom He foreknew, He also predestined to
> become conformed to the image of His Son, so that He
> would be the firstborn among many brethren; and these
> whom He predestined, He also called; and these whom
> He called, He also justified; and these whom He
> justified, He also glorified.***
>
> *– Romans 8:29-30 (NASB)*

THAT'S IT!!! Believers are put in right standing with God the Father so they can become the image of God the Son! There is a method to the madness after all! This Jesus-as-Savior stuff was designed so that you would ***be conformed to the image of His Son***, to become like Jesus. That's the point of being saved!

The Apostle Paul strived for such a Christ-likeness. He wrote about it in Philippians Chapter 3. He even went so far as stating those who wish to be like Christ should try to focus on being as perfectly obedient to God as Jesus was.

> ***Not that I have already obtained it or have already become
> perfect, but I press on so that I may lay hold of that for
> which also I was laid hold of by Christ Jesus. Brethren, I
> do not regard myself as having laid hold of it yet; but one
> thing I do: forgetting what lies behind and reaching forward
> to what lies ahead, I press on toward the goal for the prize
> of the upward call of God in Christ Jesus. Let us therefore,
> as many as are perfect, have this attitude.***
>
> *– Philippians 3:12-15 (NASB)*

The reason Jesus laid hold of each Believer and that prize in Philippians 3, is what Paul refers to in Romans 8:29; God's molding the Believer into to the likeness of His Son.

God sacrificed His Son and Jesus sacrificed Himself for you to be like Him. Paul presses on or struggles (or fights or perseveres or whatever verb you want to use) to let you know that this is his singular goal in life—and it should be the singular goal of EVERY Believer.

Yeah, I know. Even if you've gone to church, it's unlikely you heard this from the pulpit. *You were made righteous to conform your life, thoughts, words, and deeds, to be JUST LIKE JESUS CHRIST.* You might have heard the word sanctification. You might even have heard it explained, and rightly so, as being set apart, made holy. What does that mean in practical terms? For *real*? TO BE JUST LIKE JESUS CHRIST! I don't know why the preacher just doesn't come out and say that. Perhaps it puts too much pressure on us Christians to:

> **As obedient children, do not conform to the evil desires**
> **you had when you lived in ignorance...; for it is written:**
> **"Be holy, because I am holy."**
>
> — 1 Peter 1:14,16 (NIV)

Well, how holy is that?

> **You therefore must be perfect, as your Heavenly**
> **Father is perfect.**
>
> — Matthew 5:48 (ESV)

Perfect? How's that possible?

> **Keep on being obedient to the word, and not merely**
> **being hearers who deceive themselves.**
>
> — James 1:22 (ISV)

Do what the word says? What does that mean?

> *"Therefore be imitators of God, as beloved children; and*
> *walk in love, just as Christ also loved you and gave Himself*
> *up for us, an offering and a sacrifice to God as a fragrant*
> *aroma.*
>
> – Ephesians 5:1 (NASB)

Or, as the Apostle Paul stated,

> *Be imitators of me, just as I also am of Christ.*
>
> – 1 Corinthians 11:1 (NASB)

Summing up that scriptural bum rush, the more you read, study, and meditate on the Bible, and then put into practice, the more you see the glory of Christ. That sight with an unobstructed view, turns you, a step, a day, an instance, a circumstance at a time, by the power of the Holy Spirit, into Christ's likeness (2 Corinthians 3:18). You will be like Him. I know, I know, it's—mystical. *But anywho, that's the real on why God saved you.* Next question. Yes, you in the back.

"Hey, didn't Christ fix all that sinning stuff when He saved me?" Yes, in more ways than you think. This fixing wasn't just an external thing. He didn't just fix sins with God. Christ fixes you internally. If you truly want to be right with God the Father, by allowing Christ, God the Son, to put you in right standing, then God the Holy Spirit comes into you and changes the way you think.

> *Do not be conformed to this world, but be transformed*
> *by the renewal of your mind.*
>
> – Romans 12:2 (ESV)

> ***When the Spirit of truth comes, he will guide you into***
> ***all the truth….***
>
> – John 16:13 (ESV)

Now don't get this twisted; it's not a complete brain transplant. The old "You" is still hanging around in there. But there was a reason you came to Christ in the first place. The main reason is that you wanted a better life than the old You produced. You wanted to do something different, BE something different, right? Why else would you have shown up at Christ's door? *If you ain't sick, you don't need a doctor, right?* Hello? Stay with me here.

So if you want a different life, if you want to be right with God, you have to change your mindset to conform to what God wants. *If you keep doin' what cha doin', you'll keep* (all together now) *gettin' what cha gettin'! If you want something different,* (you all know the words) *you gotta do something different!* And what *difference* does God want from you? Perfection.

What God wants is for you not to be influenced by your old life in the world but to be shaped to a new life, in the shape of His perfectly-obedient Son. Of course, you have zero ability to do that on your own. That's why you need Christ as Lord, to teach you the way, to give you that shape, a pattern, a backdrop. He is a leader to guide you down the correct path. Because you can't do it on your own, God does it for you…kinda. Remember Ezekiel 36:26 and the new heart?

He gives you a new mindset, one that is attuned to what He wants and how He wants it. His mindset in you is patterned after Christ and powered by the Holy Spirit. But it is activated by…YOU. This whole concept of sanctification, of being like Christ, is like a light switch. You can have all the power the power company can create flowing through the wires, but it doesn't matter one bit if you don't flip the switch. If you want to change, you gotta have the *will* to change. God gives you all the tools and all the power, but it's up to you to put in the work—kinda.

God looks at the Believer and sees the perfection of Christ. That's the justification part again. You are justified by the perfection Christ gave your acceptance of His sacrifice. That is called *imputation*.

> ***"Imputation is used to designate any action or word or thing
> as reckoned to a person."***
>
> – *Bible Study Tools*

Christ *reckoned*, or put in the Believer's spiritual bank account, His perfect obedience. However, while the Believer has the imputed righteousness, he must also have a practical righteousness. He has to practice what has been bestowed upon him; you have to show you've got that perfection in your account. Now God, knowing your perfection-generating abilities apart from Him are zero, helps a brother out:

> ***...work out your own salvation with fear and trembling,
> for it is God who is at work in you, both to will and to
> work for His good pleasure.***
>
> – Philippians 2:12-13

God works and you work. He puts it in, you work it out. He works on you; you work on you. You both work to make you more and more like Christ. This concept is so foreign today it might as well be a different language. Perhaps this is why people do not see, or want, the value of Christ as Lord. His true value is present only if you want to be like Him, if you truly want to obey God as perfectly as you can.

If you are interested in knowing more (and I take it you are because you're still reading), let's see just how this whole process of conforming-you-to-the-likeness-of-Christ thing, this ***good pleasure***, is accomplished. We will look at three aspects of Jesus as Lord:

1....as Master,

2....as Teacher, and

3....as King.

Jesus Christ as Master

When I think of having a master, or being under the rule of someone else, I chafe. I want to be my own person in control of my own destiny. So what does it mean to have Jesus as my Master? What is the cost, and what is the benefit?

In Luke Chapter 5, we see the apostle Peter begin to follow Jesus and regard him as Master. Jesus is preaching on the seashore, and a fisherman named Peter listens as he mends his nets. When Jesus finishes preaching, He turns to Peter and tells him to put his boats out into the deep part of the sea and catch fish. Peter responds, saying they've been fishing all night and haven't caught anything. But because Jesus commands, they put the boats out.

When Peter and his partners cast their nets, they catch so many fish that the boat begins to sink. Peter turns to Jesus, and says, "Leave me! For I am a sinful man, Lord!" Jesus looks at Peter with love, and says, "Do not be afraid. From now on you will be catching men." And Peter leaves his nets and follows Jesus.

So what did it cost Peter to follow Jesus as his Master? Peter responded to Jesus as Master in two ways: first, by obedience. When Jesus told Peter to take the boats out into the deep and catch fish, it made no sense—typically fishermen would fish at night in the shoals where the fish gathered. Jesus gave bad fishing advice! But Peter responded with obedience—even though he was skeptical.

Second, Peter responded to Jesus as Master with submission—by leaving the fish he just caught, putting down his nets, and following Jesus.

What was the benefit for Peter to follow Jesus? The benefit was life transformation. Peter said, "Depart from me, for I am a sinful man," but Jesus responded, "Do not be afraid; from now on you will catch men." Peter recognized his sin and Jesus's holiness; the two cannot mix.

Peter was afraid that his sin would contaminate Jesus. Peter didn't know that Jesus could purify man's sin and cover his shame. Jesus wasn't contaminated, Peter was purified. Jesus transformed Peter's life. Christ forgave sin and called Peter to a new life.

Later, in Matthew 19:27, Peter asked Jesus, "We have left everything and followed you. What then will we have?" (What is the benefit?) Jesus replied, "...everyone who has left houses or brothers or sisters or mother or children or lands for my Name's sake, will receive a hundredfold and will inherit eternal life."

Following Jesus as Master is costly—it costs us all we have. Yet the benefits are immeasurable. We receive abundant life now and eternal life to come.

– Nathan Foth

How Much Does That Cost?

"The mountain is high, the valley is low,
and you're confused on which way to go.
So I've come here to give you a hand and
lead you into the promised land.
So, come on and take a free ride."

– Edgar Winter, *Free Ride*

For you know that it was not with perishable things such
as silver or gold that you were redeemed from the empty
way of life handed down to you from your ancestors, but
with the precious blood of Christ, a lamb without
blemish or defect.

– 1 Peter 1:18-19 (NIV)

Have you ever heard that salvation is free? Whoever told you that didn't know what they were talking about. Salvation costs...a lot. It was not free for Jesus and it will not be free for the Believer. Granted, there seems to be some disconnect between **no cost** (Revelations 21:6) and **count the cost** (Luke 14:28). Confusion about the difference is a roadblock until you understand the meaning of cost.

cost \'kȯst\: the price of something: the amount of money
that is needed to pay for or buy something

If you accept the sacrifice of Christ, if you are healed by His stripes (Isaiah 53:5), if you are reconciled to God by Christ's death on the cross, then you have a gift you could never afford.

> *Or what will a man give in exchange for his soul?*
> – Matthew 16:26 (NASB)

Man doesn't have anything he could use to pay God for salvation (Psalm 50:12). But salvation costs something; a lot in fact, the death of Jesus. Man's obedience to Christ is as much payment for salvation as the biblical animal sacrifices of old. The Believer's obedience does not pay for salvation. It is a gift of love from Man to God, just as salvation is a love gift from God to Man (John 3:16, Ephesians 2:8).

Because God was merciful to a Believer in giving him the opportunity to become friends with Him and not holding his sins against him, the least the ex-sinner could do to acknowledge the great sacrifice of Jesus Christ is to sacrifice his life. That's right, to be a Believer will require *your* life: *your* hopes, *your* dreams, *your* desires, *your* opinions, *your* viewpoints, *your* comfort, *your*…. In short, the cost of God's gift is *yourself.*

> *Therefore I urge you, brethren, by the mercies of God, to*
> *present your bodies a living and holy sacrifice, acceptable*
> *to God, which is your spiritual service of worship.*
> – Romans 12:1 (NASB)

So, where does this sacrifice begin?

Out With The Old, In With The New.

"If you are content with the old world, try to preserve it, it is very sick and will not hold out much longer. But if you cannot bear to live in everlasting dissonance between your beliefs and your life, thinking one thing and doing another, get out…."

– Alexander Ivanovich Herzen, Russian writer and thinker

Therefore, if anyone is in Christ, he is a new creation. The old has passed away; behold, the new has come.

– 2 Corinthians 5:17 (ESV)

That new creation is a slave—to Christ. God has created a new spiritual creature inside your same body. You might look the same on the outside, but you are new on the inside. You don't think the same way, want the same things, or react in the same way. You are obedient to the commands of God presented in the Bible.

Okay, let's not take this the wrong way. No, there's no electric shock, no bang on the forehead and you fall to the floor, no voice from the heavens claiming, "Luke, I'm your father" (*little Star Wars humor in there…uh… sorry*). No, you initially become a slave to Christ in your thinking.

Your *perspective*, or point of view, changes. Things that were important before will begin to mean little to you. You will have a longer-term time horizon, an *eternal* view of things. You will decide that what Christ wants is what you want. So why do people say salvation is free?

Because they didn't work for it. They didn't earn it. But make no mistake; just because you didn't earn it doesn't mean that you're not going to have to work. It's like this: Christ paid the price for your disobedience so that you could go to work for Him. In the Scriptures, this transaction looks like this:

*God saved you by his grace when you believed. And you
can't take credit for this; it is a gift from God. Salvation
is not a reward for the good things we have done, so none
of us can boast about it. For we are God's masterpiece.
He has created us anew in Christ Jesus, so we can do the
good things he planned for us long ago.*

– Ephesians 2:8-10 (NLT)

Folks, free ain't *free*. Justification wasn't free for Jesus, and sanctification is not going to be easy for the Believer (more on that later). Now let's see how that change of perspective takes place.

I Think It Makes It So.

"I think therefore I am."

– Rene Descartes,
French philosopher, mathematician, and scientist

For as he thinks within himself, so he is.

– Proverb 23:7 (NASB)

Put yourself in the shoes of a Believer. Remember when we talked about how justification (being in right-standing with God) leads you to sanctification (becoming more like Christ)? Well, that becoming-more-like-Christ part shows itself first in the way a Believer thinks. You think as Jesus thought. And how is that?

*Jesus said to them, "My food is to do the will of him who
sent me and to accomplish his work."*

– John 4:34 (NASB)

> *Now is my soul troubled. And what shall I say? "Father,*
> *save me from this hour"? But for this purpose I have*
> *come to this hour.*
>
> – John 12:27 (NASB)

> *"…I say as the Father has told Me."*
>
> – John 12:50 (NASB)

See a recurring theme here? For those of you not good at *Where's Waldo*, the theme is obedience. Jesus, God the Son, obeyed God the Father completely, without complaint. In a word, He obeyed *perfectly*. That's what God wants from you. He wants you to become the likeness of His Son, as perfectly obedient as His Son was. That's why He wants to save you.

That's why Jesus died for you. That's the whole point of justification. That is the essence of sanctification. That is the work of the Holy Spirit. OBEDIENCE. To what extent is the cost of this obedience to Jesus Christ as Master? The obedience of a slave. If you would stay with me here for just a few minutes, let's get into a little Bible translation.

The Greek word for servant in this passage is doulou (or doulos). Interesting word, doulos; it means slave. Yeah, I know the interpretation uses "servant." In other Bible passages doulos is translated as "bondservant." However, the word doulos means slave. Consider the definitions below.

doo' - loss

1. a slave, bondman, man of servile condition

a. a slave

b. metaph., one who gives himself up to another's will, those whose service is used by Christ in extending and advancing his cause among men

c. devoted to another to the disregard of one's own interests

– The KJV New Testament Greek Lexicon

Doulos: a slave

– Strong's Greek Lexicon

doúlos (a masculine noun of uncertain derivation) – properly, someone who belongs to another; a bond-slave, without any ownership rights of their own.

– HELPS Word-studies

Doulos: a slave

– NAS Concordance

"Question: What is a bondservant / bond-servant?
Answer: A bondservant is a slave. In some Bibles the
word bondservant is the translation of the Greek word doulos,
which means "one who is subservient to, and entirely at the
disposal of, his master; a slave." Other translations use the
word slave or servant. In Roman times, the term bondservant
or slave could refer to someone who voluntarily served others.
But it usually referred to one who was held in a permanent
position of servitude. Under Roman law, a bondservant was
considered the owner's personal property. Slaves essentially
had no rights and could even be killed with impunity
(without punishment) by their owners."
– http://www.gotquestions.org/bondservant.html

Dude, doulos means slave. And just as Jesus came to Earth in the form of a man, a slave to God the Father (Philippians 2:7), Believers are to imitate Jesus's obedience by being His slave. BELIEVERS ARE SLAVES TO CHRIST. We do only what He tells us to do. If we do not do what we are told to do, or we do what we are told not to do, we are disobedient slaves. But slaves, nonetheless, we are.

Above, Nathan Foth wrote, "When I think of having a master, or being under the rule of someone else, I chafe." Ouch! The kind of slavery spoken of here is not the fresh-off-the-boat-welcome-to-the-neighborhood-love-American-style slavery. No— this master isn't into whips, hobbling, rapes, castrations, starvation, denigration, spitting, torturing…. (I think you get the point by now.) This is a different kind of slavery.

First, let's think about how a Believer came to be a slave. They were purchased. No, they didn't stand on the block in Charleston, South Carolina, sold to the highest bidder. Christ purchased every Believer from Satan.

> *Do you not know that if you present yourselves to*
> *anyone as obedient slaves, you are slaves of the one*
> *whom you obey, either of sin, which leads to death,*
> *or of obedience, which leads to righteousness?*
>
> – Romans 6:16

> *Do you not know that your bodies are temples of the*
> *Holy Spirit, who is in you, whom you have received from*
> *God? You are not your own; you were bought at a price….*
>
> – 1 Corinthians 6:19-20 (NIV)

The Believer once obeyed Satan: he was Satan's slave. Christ bought that Believer from Satan at the price of Christ's blood. (1 Peter 1:18-19)

What slave owner back in the day purchased his slaves with his own life? Kinda defeats the purpose, doesn't it? I mean, you got a bunch of slaves, but you're not around to command them to get stuff done for you? No, salvation is a very different kind of slavery. You belong to Christ because He purchased you with His death. He paid your debt of sin and now you belong to Him. Simple as that.

"But I don't feel any different." That's what many (if not most) people say about salvation. You didn't grow wings or anything outwardly miraculous. That's because the transformation into slavery starts inside, with the mind.

This or That.

> *"You can get with this, or you can get with that. I think you'll get with this, for this is where it's at."*
>
> – Black Sheep, *The Choice is Yours*

> *You adulterous people, don't you know that friendship with the world means enmity against God? Therefore, anyone who chooses to be a friend of the world becomes an enemy of God.*
>
> – James 4:4 (NIV)

To be a Believer, you first become a slave to Christ in the way you think about life. Whether you acknowledge it or not, you are a *me-first* person. We, as humans, all are. Even when we do something we deem good, we do it to make ourselves feel better about—ourselves! See what a generous, kind, loving, selfish, self-promoting, God-hating, Christ-denying person I am?

"But…but…I don't hate God or Christ." That's not quite the way the Bible sees it.

> *For he who is not with me is against me.*
>
> – Luke 11:23 (NASB)

> *No one can serve two masters, for either he will hate the*
> *one and love the other, or he will be devoted to the*
> *one and despise the other.*
>
> – Matthew 6:24

Choose.

Like when you were a kid at the store and your momma said you can have vanilla or strawberry ice cream and you said—*both*. Uh…it doesn't *quite* work like that with Christ. He didn't die to save your life so you could do whatever you want for eternity.

No sir, you don't get to obey Him sometimes and do what you want sometimes, with one foot in Heaven and one foot on Earth. He saved you to serve Him to the extent a slave would serve a master.

Don't get all chafed thinking about being a slave to Christ. If you're not saved, you're currently a slave to Satan. When you don't come to Christ, admit your sins, and turn from wanting to be disobedient to wanting to be obedient (repenting), you are doing exactly what Satan wants you to do. When you want all the things this world has to offer, the lust of the eyes, the lust of the flesh, and the pride of life (1 John 2:16), you are obeying Satan. And because you can't be a slave to two masters (Matthews 6:24), you are either a slave to Christ or a slave to Satan.

That's salvation. You are coming out of Satan's control and into the control of Christ. You choose Christ as your Master instead of Satan. Christ commands you rather than Satan. And let's make this perfectly clear. IF YOU HAVE NOT COMMITTED YOUR LIFE TO CHRIST, YOU HAVE COMMITTED IT TO SATAN—*PERIOD*!

To paraphrase another story I heard:

There was a softball game between a team picked by Satan and one picked by Christ. But the best player didn't want to play for either, so he decided to sit on the fence and watch. When the game was over, Satan's team packed up and went back to Hell, and Christ's team returned to Heaven. Satan walked up to the guy on the fence and said, "Let's go." The guy said, "Wait, I didn't play for you; I sat on this fence." Satan replied, "Yeah but it's my fence."

There's no fence-sitting with salvation. You're either a *saint* or *you ain't*.

Bottom line? When you commit your thinking to being obedient to the Word of God, you are truly a slave to Christ.

> *We destroy arguments and every lofty opinion raised*
> *against the knowledge of God, and take every thought*
> *captive to obey Christ….*
>
> – 2 Corinthians 10:5-6

If I Could Be Like….

> *"Imitation is the greatest form of flattery."*
> – Charles Caleb Cotton, English cleric, writer and collector

> *Be imitators of me as I also am of Christ.*
> – 1 Corinthians 11:1

"But why do I need to be a *slave*?" Three reasons: (1) If you're going to become the likeness of Jesus and *He* was a slave, *you* have to be a slave, (2) Perfection requires obedience—complete, total, unwavering obedience—forever, and (3) the provision that comes from the Master.

If your desire is to be like Christ, and He was a slave to God the Father, should you want less? For the remainder of his life on Earth, the Believer is being pressed in the model of Jesus Christ, the exact representation of God (Hebrews 1:3). And you, as a Believer, will be modeled, to a lesser degree, into the representation of Jesus. That's the plan. To aid in its completion requires the mindset of a slave.

This slave/master relationship might become more clear to you when you realize what being a Christian, a true Believer in Christ, means. It means sacrifice.

> **he (Jesus Christ) made himself nothing by taking the very**
> **nature of a servant, being made in human likeness ...**
>
> – Philippians 2:7(NIV)

Exactly how can you **make yourself nothing**, to give up the world's contamination? How do you give up your hopes, your dreams, your desires, your opinions, and your viewpoints? Yeah, that's right, you can't. You see, folks, when you come to Christ, there's going to be war going on inside you; a war of wills, a war for your soul.

> **For the desires of the flesh are against the Spirit, and the**
> **desires of the Spirit are against the flesh, for these are**
> **opposed to each other, to keep you from doing the**
> **things you want to do.**
>
> – Galatians 5:17 (ESV)

Kinda reminds me of a Looney Tunes cartoon song. (Sorry, I know it dates me, but those were/are some GREAT cartoons with outstanding songs!). A can of 50/50 Pipe Tobacco sings:

> **"Half of me says let's get religion, half of me says no we won't.**
> **Good Lord, I'm in a mess of trouble. Half of me wants to be**
> **good; only half of me wants to be good."**
>
> – *Little Blabbermouse* (1940)

I probably haven't seen that cartoon in more than thirty years, yet I still remember that song. Perhaps it foretold of things to come in my life. But anywho....

That's the war that's going to take place in your life as long as you're a Believer on this Earth. Sometimes you do right; sometimes you do wrong. But how do you create the *will* to do right, or at least want to do right?

Promises, Promises.

> *"I beg your pardon, I never promised you a rose garden. Along*
> *with the sunshine there's gotta be a little rain sometimes."*
> – Lynn Anderson, *I Never Promised You A Rose Garden*

> *Shall we accept good from God, and not trouble?*
> – Job 2:10 (NIV)

God knows how weak Man is, even in his renewed state. Our Master understands the battle that goes on. However, that does not lessen the command for Believers to be totally obedient, regardless of the cost. *'Cause for some reason, folks been spreadin' lies 'bout the Christian life.* Wine and roses, strawberries and cream, kittens and babies? **Don't you believe it**! If we are to be like Christ, what should we expect?

> *"A servant (doulos: slave) is not greater than his master. If*
> *they persecuted me, they will also persecute you."*
> – John 15:20 (NASB)

Jesus said you should expect to be persecuted for your obedience.

> *He was despised and rejected by others, and a man of*
> *sorrows, intimately familiar with suffering.*
> – Isaiah 53:3 (ISV)

You should expect to be despised and rejected—and most of all:

> **And after you have suffered a little while, the God of all**
> **grace, who has called you to his eternal glory in Christ,**
> **will himself restore, confirm, strengthen, and establish**
> **you.**
>
> – 1 Peter 5:10

BELIEVERS IN JESUS CHRIST AS LORD SHOULD EXPECT TO **_SUFFER_**!!!

None of that sounds like wine and roses to me. And it didn't look that way to the apostle Paul, either. You know, the guy who wrote thirteen books (maybe fourteen, if you count Hebrews) of the New Testament? The guy who wanted to be like Christ more than anything else in the world? Well…

In 2 Corinthians 11:24-25, Paul provides a list of a few items of cost for his slavish devotion to Christ.

- Put in prison (a bunch of times) – CHECK!

- Whipped (a lot) – CHECK!

- Thirty-nine lashes (five times) – CHECK!

- Beaten with rods (three times) – CHECK!

- Stoned (only once) – CHECK!

- Shipwrecked (three times) – CHECK!

- Adrift at sea (a night and a day) – CHECK!

Talk about adding up the cost of Jesus Christ as Lord! Get the picture? No? Well, Paul doesn't want anyone reading about His life to get it twisted, so…

> *I have traveled on many long journeys. I have faced danger
> from rivers and from robbers. I have faced danger from my
> own people, the Jews, as well as from the Gentiles. I have
> faced danger in the cities, in the deserts, and on the
> seas. And I have faced danger from men who claim to be
> believers but are not. I have worked hard and long, enduring
> many sleepless nights. I have been hungry and thirsty and
> have often gone without food. I have shivered in the cold,
> without enough clothing to keep me warm. Then, besides
> all this, I have the daily burden of my concern for all the churches.*
>
> – 2 Corinthians 11:26-28

Now straight up, does that sound like the kind of party you wanna get an invite to? Sign me up…uh…No?! I don't know about you, but Paul's life doesn't sound like one I would run into headlong. And that's the theme of suffering. You are going to have to do some things you don't really want to do and not do some things you really want to do. Why? Because that fight between the flesh and the spirit aren't just internal.

Remember 1 John 2:16 (ESV):

> *For all that is in the world—the desires of the flesh and
> the desires of the eyes and pride of life—is not from the
> Father but is from the world.*

The unsaved part of you, the "flesh" part of you, still wants the stuff the world lusts for. And so does the whole unsaved world! So when you deny that lust, you're going to suffer. The flesh part of you, or the "unredeemed" part of you, will try to get you to give in and "enjoy" the world. The world's likes and dislikes are just the opposite of God's. Basically the world just wants to disobey God.

Simply put:

1. Believers are aligned with what God wants.

2. Non-Believers are aligned with what Satan wants (which is whatever God *doesn't* want).

3. Therefore, to be aligned with God is to align against the world, and

4. If you are aligned against the world, the world will make you suffer.

Commercials, popular music, movies, entertainment, sports… whatever cultural display you come in contact with can be used against the purity and perfection of God found in Jesus Christ. And that impurity will be exactly what the unredeemed flesh (and the unredeemed world) will be for. Jesus even told this to His worldly brothers:

> *For not even his brothers believed in him. Jesus said to them, "My time has not yet come, but your time is always here. The world cannot hate you, but it hates me because I testify about it that its works are evil."*
>
> – John 7: 5-7 (ESV)

> *"Because Jesus's brothers did not believe Him, they were of the world and therefore knew nothing of God or His purposes."*
>
> – John MacArthur Study Bible

"Brother Can You Spare a Dime?"

> *"I still really, really love you. Love is stronger than pride."*
>
> – Sade, *Love Is Stronger Than Pride*

> *"And Jesus said to him, "The foxes have holes and the*
> *birds of the air have nests, but the Son of Man has*
> *nowhere to lay His head.""*
>
> – Luke 9:58 (NASB)

It's going to take a certain mindset to fight the world that's in you and the world outside of you. And that mindset is going to create suffering and require obedience. It might even mean that you will be deprived of something you think you need. Maybe you lose your job, or your home, or some other necessity. This is when having a slave mentality REALLY helps.

Remember when we talked about the difference between the mentality of slavery in biblical times and the slavery in a western European setting? While not a garden party, the slavery of the Bible did have an interesting tint on the relationship between master and slave.

> *Masters, provide your slaves with what is right and fair,*
> *because you know that you also have a Master in heaven.*
>
> – Colossians 4:1(NIV)

Right and fair; interesting concepts, especially when they are applied to slavery. But there it is, in black and white. Masters are supposed to take care of their slaves. In his book, *Slave*, John MacArthur gives us a look at the biblical relationship between master and slave:

> *"Slaves did not have to worry about where their next meal would*
> *come from or whether or not they would have a place to stay.*
> *Their sole concern was to carry out the interests of their owner.*
> *In return the master cared for their needs."*

Sounds reasonable, right? Here's the tricky part: Who gets to decide what the slave "needs"? Okay, time's up— it's the master. Whatever you don't have, it's because the master decided you didn't need it. Can you see where this discussion is headed?

To be a slave to Christ means *He* decides what you need and when you need it to fulfill the work you are supposed to be doing for Him. Christ packs your lunch (Philippians 4:19), and you don't get to grumble and complain when you don't get pudding (Philippians 2:14). From the state of Christianity today, I know this might come as a shock to most Christians; but hey, don't shoot me. I'm just the messenger.

Most Christians today believe God owes them something, at least a "reasonable" living. I'd like to know where His word says that. No, what Christians display is pride. "I'm one of your chosen, so I deserve this and I deserve that." Now let's think about this for a sec. Can you imagine a slave telling his master what the slave deserves? How do you think that conversation would end? You do understand that as a slave, your worth is determined by what the Master gains? And what exactly would that be?

> *So likewise ye, when ye shall have done all those things*
> *which are commanded you, say, We are unprofitable*
> *servants (slaves): we have done that which was our duty*
> *to do.*
>
> – Luke 17:10 (KJV)

Unprofitable. *You've gained God…let me see…add the 6…carry the 4…uh… NOTHING!* As a loyal, obedient slave, whatever you do for God is whatever you were supposed to do for God. It's your job. And God gives you what you need to do His work.

Ladies and gentlemen, being a slave to Christ means allowing Him to provide for you. Not the manna-from-heaven type provision, you must have the will to work (2 Thessalonians 3:10). But one thing should be clear, Christ said He'd be with Believers always (Matthew 28:20). So when you don't have this or you don't have that, even if it's something like food, or shelter or clothing, know that the

Master is there. You must have a slave's mentality: *If the Master did not provide it for me, then I must not need it for what He wants me to do*. Paul sums it up like this:

> **Not that I am speaking of being in need, for I have learned in whatever situation I am to be content. I know how to be brought low, and I know how to abound. In any and every circumstance, I have learned the secret of facing plenty and hunger, abundance and need. I can do all things through him who strengthens me.**
>
> – Philippians 4:11-13

That's why you need to think like a slave, to the level of slavish devotion. Otherwise, the suffering will get the best of even the strongest Believer. So when things don't go his way, the obedient slave has the mindset that *I do what my master commands, and I live with the result.*

"Obey God and leave all the consequences to Him."
> – Rev. Dr. Charles Stanley, American pastor and author

That's called love. Caring enough to sacrifice. Everything. Unto death.

All We Need is Love.

> **"There nothing you can do that can't be done.**
> **Nothing you can sing that can't be sung.**
> **Nothing you can say, but you can learn how to play the game….**
> **All you need is love, love. Love is all we need."**
>
> – The Beatles, *All You Need is Love*

> ***And being found in human form, he humbled himself***
> ***by becoming obedient to the point of death, even death***
> ***on a cross.***
>
> – Philippians 2:8 (ESV)

God the Son loved God the Father so much that He was obedient, even unto death. Death in the most shameful and humiliating way possible. Now THAT'S a slave.

Jesus's example of obedience illustrates why Believers have to have the mindset of a slave; to focus on the love of Christ and their love for Christ. You don't know what Jesus has for you to do. You don't know where you might have to go, what you might have to endure, or to whom you might have to speak. Remember, your life is no longer your own.

> ***I have been crucified with Christ; and it is no longer I***
> ***who live, but Christ lives in me; and the life which I***
> ***now live in the flesh I live by faith in the Son of God,***
> ***who loved me and gave Himself up for me.***
>
> – Galatians 2:20 (NASB)

Remember, you were bought from Satan with the blood of Christ to become a willing participant (okay, a bondservant, if that makes you feel better, a willing slave) in what He wants. That's how much He cared about you. He cared enough to sacrifice His life.

And the only way Believers can have the practical will to care enough to sacrifice their own lives, to love Christ in return, is to have a slavish devotion. To what? To obeying the commands of Christ in the Bible—no matter the cost, even to the point of death. That is what it means to be a slave to Christ.

As Believer, if things aren't going *your* way, the way you think things should (or the way you want them to), perhaps you need to understand that, if you are obedient to the Word of God, things are going *God's* way. Remember *not my will but Yours be done*? If this is to be the Believer's mindset, then perhaps this is an appropriate prayer:

> *"Lord, help me not to get what I want, but to want what I get."*

YOU ARE HERE TO DO WHAT GOD WANTS; HE IS NOT HERE TO DO WHAT YOU WANT!!!

Isn't that what Jesus said?

> *For I have come down from Heaven, not to do my own*
> *will but the will of him who sent me.*
>
> – John 6:38 (NASB)

To sacrifice unconditional obedience to Christ, to love the Son, just as the Son loved the Father, is the mindset of a slave. That's what God expected from Jesus, the Son of Man, that's what Jesus expects from the Believer, and that's what the Master expects from His slaves. If you can't get with that, you might want to look for another religion. That's the cost of Jesus Christ as Master.

But don't get discouraged. Jesus provides the Believer with resources.

> *But the Helper, the Holy Spirit, whom the Father will*
> *send in my name, he will teach you all things and bring*
> *to your remembrance all that I have said to you.*
>
> – John 14:26 (ESV)

Believers will learn how to be a slave to Christ. The Holy Spirit of Christ will provide the power for them to learn at the feet of Jesus, the Teacher.

Jesus Christ as Teacher

Let us define what a teacher is and review the good qualities of someone in that position. But let us first review what to teach means, as defined by www.oxforddictionaries.com. To teach "is to impart knowledge to or instruct (someone) as to how to do something."

So a teacher's function is to share knowledge. Now let's all think back to a teacher in our own lives. We all have had at least one whom we considered a good teacher. What were some of that teacher's qualities? I will list as many as I can think of, drawing from my own experiences.

- Was inspirational

- Offered sound guidance

- Provided leadership

- Armed me for trials and tests to come

- Set an example for how to do things correctly

- Empowered their students (making students stronger and more confident)

- Illustrated selflessness

- Acted authoritative

- Lived humbly

- Took ownership of my academic growth

- Came to my level to bring me up to theirs

Let's now turn to how this relates to Christ as Teacher. The above qualities are each fantastic for a teacher, and one who possessed several would be considered a gifted teacher. How much more valuable would these qualities be if they were found in a single Being, one who is infinitely more knowledgeable than all teachers past, present, and future combined?

In Christ Jesus, we find all of the qualities listed above and more. In the Bible, we see that God came down to Earth and lived among mankind in human form. Then at the appointed time, God the Son became the greatest Teacher ever to be. Throughout the Gospels, Christ the Teacher showed the world God and His person.

In each of the Gospels, the Books of Matthew, Mark, Luke, and John, we learn that God the Son came down from Heaven in the form of a baby, born and reared from a child to a man. Then He began to teach mankind about the Kingdom of Heaven and about God the Father as only the Son could.

During His journey back to Heaven, Christ the Teacher expounded on the truth about life, the Scriptures, and mankind's fallen nature, imploring all to deny themselves and follow His example. Each Gospel ends with the Teacher being the ultimate example so that one day we would have a sinless nature like Him.

Now how great is our God? He didn't have to do any of that and would be completely justified in not doing so. Let us not forget that time after time He has warned mankind through His prophets and angels, unleashing judgment when people failed to heed his warnings.

Knowing the reception His Son would receive from the majority of people on Earth, the Godhead still sent the Teacher who accepted His role and perfectly showed (taught) us the way to salvation.

– Jonathan D'Mario Williams

When in Doubt, Read the Instructions.

*"The whole art of teaching is only the art of awakening the
natural curiosity of the mind for the purpose of
satisfying it afterwards."*

– Anatole France. French poet, journalist, and novelist

*Then Philip ran up to the chariot and heard the man
reading Isaiah the prophet. "Do you understand what you
are reading?" Philip asked. "How can I," he said, "unless
someone explains it to me?"*

– Acts 8:30-31

Ahhh—you want to be a slave, do you? Maybe, maybe not. I take it that if you've gotten this far in the book that you want to know more. And if there is one subject that any person interested in Christianity should want more info on, it's where to find instructions on how to be a good slave. I've got what they need. The Bible is just such an instruction manual (2 Timothy 3:16).

In short, the Bible tells you everything you need to know about how to be an obedient slave. It is the textbook of slavery. It is Basic Instructions Before Leaving Earth for the slave of Christ. But there's one little problem. Like most textbooks, the Bible is limited in its usefulness by the teacher who aids in the application of its information.

Like the man in the opening verses above, Believers need someone to help them interpret the instruction manual (the B.I.B.L.E.). And who better to aid you in the study of being an obedient slave than the most obedient slave who ever lived? And that would be... (okay this isn't a pop quiz, but you *did* read the last chapter, right?) Jesus Christ!

The greatness of the Bible, especially the New Testament, is that it teaches how to be a slave by revealing how the great Teacher taught. And while He taught on being a slave, Jesus also set the example by being a slave (more on that later in the chapter). That's what Jesus did with His disciples.

disciple dis·ci·ple \di-ˈsī-pəl\: someone who accepts and
helps to spread the teachings of a famous person

— Merriam-Webster Dictionary

But for the purposes of this book, let's get a little more in-depth definition:

"a scholar, sometimes applied ... principally to the followers of
Christ. A disciple of Christ is one who
(1) believes his doctrine,
(2) rests on his sacrifice,
(3) imbibes ("drinks in") his spirit, and
(4) imitates his example...."

— Easton Bible Dictionary

Or simply, you're a disciple if you wanna be taught the ways of being a slave to Jesus Christ. I know, I know, if you've heard the term described at all, that wasn't the way you heard it. Nevertheless, that's what it says in the Bible. Remember what we discussed in the past chapter about being a slave?

In the introduction, Jonathan D'Mario Williams told us above that Christ the Teacher expounds upon the truth about life, about the Scriptures and about mankind's fallen nature, imploring all to deny themselves and follow His example.

Then Jesus said to his disciples, "Whoever wants to be my
disciple must deny themselves and take up their cross and
follow me."

— Matthew 16:24 (NIV)

There are three parts to being a disciple:

1. ***Deny yourself*** – being content with not always getting what you want

2. ***Pick up your cross*** – being content with (more often than not) getting what you do not want

3. ***Follow me*** – doing what Jesus did the way He teaches it through the B.I.B.L.E.

The first two parts are clearly slave talk, and the third is slave turned student. Following Jesus is about listening and obeying, being a slave not only to His commands but to His teaching. And that, friend, is the beautiful symmetry of being a disciple of Jesus Christ. He demands obedience and then teaches how to be obedient. So often people claim to be followers of Jesus, disciples of Jesus, yet know very little of the instruction manual, the Bible.

The "Why" Before the "What."

> *"Start with Why."*
> – Simon Sinek, author, speaker, and consultant

> ***Teach me Your way, O LORD; I will walk in Your truth….***
> – Psalms 86:11 (NASB)

Have you ever sat in a class and wondered: Why I gotta know this stuff? Well—that question is bound in a term called *relevance*. Merriam-Webster's definition is:

relevance rel·e·vance \'re-lə-vən(t)s\: relation to the matter at hand

Or said another way, what does this have to do with my interests?

Your interests are the reason you will pay attention to the knowledge imparted. You're interested in the subject matter. So we generally consider that the person (student) to whom the teacher is to impart knowledge actually wants to know what's being taught! The Bible states as much.

And He (Jesus) was saying, "He who has ears to hear, let him hear."
— Mark 4:9 (NASB)

Anyone who has ears should listen!
— Matthew 11:15 (HCSB)

Anyone with ears to hear should listen and understand.
— Matthew 13:9 (NLT)

He who has an ear, let him hear what the Spirit says to the churches.
— Revelation 2:17 (NASB)

You see, folks, if you're not interested in being a slave, then the teaching of Jesus is kinda in the subject pile of *Why-should-I-care*? So when people who claim to be disciples of Jesus Christ can't tell you from His instruction manual how they are to live their lives, one must seriously question (1) from *where* are they getting their instruction, and (2) from *whom* are they getting their instruction. Because those who want to be an obedient slave should want to get the most accurate information and be taught by the wisest teacher.

Right about now, I'm sure one of you sharp individuals out there is asking: "Isn't Jesus dead, risen, and gone? How can He teach me while He's in Heaven and I'm here?" Well—the Bible says something about that:

> *"... teaching them to observe all that I have commanded*
> *you. And behold, I (Jesus) am with you always, to the end*
> *of the age."*
>
> – Matthew 28:20 (ESV)

Knowing that nothing gets past your keen minds, I will address what seems to be a problem here. Jesus is in Heaven, yet He will be with Believers always. And the Holy Spirit is supposed to be teaching, yet you've just been reading about Jesus as Teacher. What gives? Well—*wait for it*—The Holy Spirit is Jesus Christ! Now stay with me here 'cause down the rabbit hole we go.

Ask *Him*. He Knows.

> *"I am not a teacher, but an awakener."*
>
> – Robert Frost, American Poet

> *But the Helper, the Holy Spirit, whom the Father will*
> *sending my name, he will teach you all things and bring*
> *to your remembrance all that I have said to you.*
>
> – John 14:26

Jesus told the disciples that He was going away but that He would send the Helper. That's how Jesus was going to be with them always, through the Holy Spirit. How does that work? Are Jesus Christ and the Holy Spirit both individual and the same?

That has to do with God being three persons, the Father, the Son, and the Holy Spirit: three distinct persons with one essence. More than that can't be explained. This is a you-gotta-have-faith thing. (Hopefully you'll learn, as a Believer, you don't have to have the entire answer for everything, thank God.) Remember Deuteronomy 29:29 (NIV)?

"The Lord our God has secrets known to no one. We are not accountable for them, but we and our children are accountable forever for all that he has revealed to us, that we may obey all the terms of these instructions."

In other words, what Believers will be held accountable for is on a need to know basis. God doesn't expect us to comprehend anything that He has not revealed. Therefore, let's place the full understanding of the Trinity in the secrets-known-to-no-one pile. Now, where were we? Oh yeah, Jesus as Teacher.

So we have Jesus teaching Believers through His Holy Spirit. And all that Jesus taught while He was on Earth has been preserved by those who had the Holy Spirit when the Bible was first written, and by those who had the Holy Spirit when the Bible was translated. And here's the kicker; you know what the Holy Spirit had Man write about?

When the Helper comes, whom I will send to you from the Father, that is the Spirit of truth who proceeds from the Father, He will testify about Me....

— John 15:26

That's right, the Holy Spirit of Christ teaches Man about Jesus Christ. How convenient. We need a teacher to instruct us in how to be more like Christ, and who do we get but the Spirit of Christ! I guess if Believers need to be a slave like Christ was, it would be best to get the training straight from the Christ Himself! But why is the Holy Spirit called the Helper? Because you're going to need *help* to do what you're going to be asked to do.

It Ain't Easy Being Green.

*"It's not that easy being green. Having to spend each day the
color of the leaves. When I think it might be easier being
red or yellow or gold or something much more colorful like that."*
– Kermit the Frog, *Being Green*

*For the gate is small and the way is narrow that leads
to life, and there are few who find it.*
– Matthew 7:14 (NASB)

It's easy to be good enough, especially when you've set the bar on what exactly *is* good enough. That bar is just low enough for you to jump over, or else you'd lower the bar until you could get over it (perhaps we should say "low" enough instead of "good" enough? But anywho….) Good enough is *soooooo* much easier to achieve. That's why it's the world's standard (more on that later). However, a good enough mentality is a tad low for Jesus Christ.

Remember that perfection stuff? There's no way we could be perfect in the eyes of God the Father without being covered by the perfection of God the Son. Well, the same perfect obedience that Jesus Christ produced in His life on Earth is the same perfect obedience He teaches in the Bible, and through the Holy Spirit, to all who call Him Savior. This is the *practical* righteousness we spoke of before: Practicing, or working out, the perfection that has been *imputed* righteousness, or that which is placed in you (Remember Philippians 2:12?).

The Spirit of Jesus Christ (1) helps those who want to be a perfect slave understand what is required and (2) assists in the fight between He, teamed with the spirit of the Believer aligned with God, against the flesh of the Believer, the part that is of Satan. (But we'll save that discussion for another time.) *That's kinda nice of Christ when you think about it.*

Jesus says Believers are to be as perfect as God Himself (Matthew 5:48). He just didn't say "Good luck with that!" and then start His ascension into Heaven on His way to playing eighteen holes at Pebble Beach. He specified what He wants from His slaves (perfection) and then sent the essence of Himself, the Helper (Holy Spirit), to teach what He wants and to help those who confess Him as Savior to be what He wants. See—kinda nice.

But don't play Jesus short. He's not a white-haired, old lady teacher that you laugh at after she walks past your desk (not that any of you fine, outstanding citizens did that when you were in grade school).

Everybody was Kung Fu Fighting.

> *"I said emotional content. Not anger! Now try again! With me!"*
> – Bruce Lee, *Enter The Dragon* (1973)

> *"AND YOU SHALL LOVE THE LORD YOUR GOD*
> *WITH ALL YOUR HEART, AND WITH ALL YOUR*
> *SOUL, AND WITH ALL YOUR MIND, AND WITH*
> *ALL YOUR STRENGTH."*
> – Mark 12:30 (NASB)

Look at Jesus as a sensei (*sin-say*). You've heard the term, I'm sure. (Okay, I'm not so sure.) Remember any Kung Fu movies? You know, the ones where there's a teacher and a bunch of students, and some guy comes and tries to get rid of the school and kills the—sensei? He is the head master, the master teacher, the guy in charge of instruction, the sensei.

Every Kung Fu movie has the sensei (ironically, sometimes called Master or Teacher) as *The Man*, the guy every student wanted to be. He was the one they listened to and wanted to please, and they wanted to be known as his students. But the sensei didn't take any—stuff.

Those martial arts students followed the teaching of the sensei without question or hesitation. If not, they got popped on the head, or worse, booted out of the school! Jesus is no joke in that area either, especially in telling us His view on love. (Down another rabbit hole we go….)

Ever heard, "Jesus is Love"? Love, Love, Love, … Love? Jesus is everybody's friend? Jesus loves rainbows and sinners (You remember sin, as in disobedience.), is the friend of unicorns and sinners (again, sinner as in the disobedient), and…. Well what exactly did Jesus say about love and friendship? I mean right out of His own mouth?

> *"If you love Me, you will keep My commandments."*
>
> – John 14:15 (NASB)

> ***"Whoever has My commandments and keeps them is the one who loves Me. The one who loves Me will be loved by My Father, and I will love him and reveal Myself to him."***
>
> – John 14:21(ESV)

> *"You are My friends if you do what I command you."*
>
> – John 15:14 (NASB)

Now straight up, do these verses, quotes from Jesus, sound like a guy who's all bunnies and hot cocoa? Not hardly. Sounds to me like a guy who has a strict set of guidelines and expects you who follow Him and to toe the line. Why? Because if you're going to be conformed to His likeness, that means you have to have the same mindset He had.

If you keep My commands you will remain in My love,
just as I have kept My Father's commands and remain
in His love.

– John 15:10 (HCSB)

No champagne and roses here, folks. Just compliance. Just obedience, plain and simple. After all, we defined love as caring enough to sacrifice. For the Believer, love means caring enough about what He teaches to be obedient to it, sacrificing what you *could* think and do (your will). Christ teaches, you learn, you do. Got it? Good. That just leaves the little subject of what exactly Jesus wants those who love Him to learn.

It's (NOT) All About Me.

"Humility is not thinking less of yourself, it's thinking of yourself less."

– C. S. Lewis, British novelist, poet, academic
medievalist, literary critic, essayist, lay
theologian, broadcaster, lecturer, and Christian apologist

"Therefore humble yourselves under the mighty hand of
God, that He may exalt you at the proper time…."

– 1 Peter 5:6

What we need to learn to be an obedient slave can be summed up in one word: *humility*. That is the word that summed up the sacrifice Christ made in coming to Earth (Philippians 2:8) But what is humility? It's definition is important, because people around church like to throw the word around, without really telling you what it means. So let's start with:

humble hum·ble \ˈhəm-bəl \: not proud : not thinking of
yourself as better than other people

– Merriam-Webster Dictionary

But that doesn't really show the true essence of humility the way Jesus portrayed it. In his Web article *What is Humility*, John Piper, American pastor, teacher and founder of desiringgod.org, lists some attributes:

1. Humility begins with a sense of subordination to God in Christ.

2. Humility does not feel a right to better treatment than Jesus got.

3. Humility asserts truth not to bolster ego with control or with triumphs in debate, but as service to Christ and love to the adversary.

4. Humility knows it is dependent on grace for all knowing and believing.

5. Humility knows it is fallible, and so considers criticism and learns from it.

And this is what Christ expects from…me? Yeah. Right.

Perfect obedience is hard. Truth be told, it's impossible. Why? Because sometimes a Believer wins against his urge to sin and sometimes he doesn't. Believers don't win when they make the decision to willfully do what the Satan-follower inside them wants to do. My will. (Remember Isaiah 14:13-14? If not, go back and read it again.)

That's just *thiiiis* much short of perfect obedience. But God applauds the attempt IF it comes from a mindset that the Believer wants to do the will of God. One motto I've created for my life:

Sometimes I win, sometimes I sin; ALWAYS I fight.

After all, Jesus knows His sheep are weak:

For we do not have a high priest who cannot sympathize with our weaknesses.
– Hebrews 4:15 (NASB)

Because Jesus knows as stated above that

...the spirit is willing, but the flesh is weak.
– Matthew 26:41 (NASB)

However, Jesus also knows how to fight the temptation of our flesh:

...but one who in every respect has been tempted as we are, yet without sin.
– Hebrews 4:15 (NASB)

And that, friend, is what we are to learn: How to engage in hand-to-hand combat with our old flesh to serve our new spirit, to deny what we want, to accept what we do not want, and follow Christ. That takes being humble, willing to say what He wants is more important than what I want (Luke 22:42).

Everything a Believer will be taught hinges on the want, the will, the striving like a long distance runner heading for the finish line (2 Timothy 2:7), to do what Jesus Christ teaches and commands. This means straining at the expense of everything else, even life itself. And there's no better teacher than the most obedient slave who ever lived, Jesus Christ.

Addition by Subtraction.

> *"Perfection is achieved, not when there is nothing more to add,*
> *but when there is nothing left to take away."*
>
> – Antoine de Saint-Exupéry, French writer, poet,
> aristocrat, journalist, and aviator

> *Hate what is evil; cling to what is good....*
>
> – Romans 12:9 (NIV)

Okay, okay, no panic, please. Everyone walk orderly to the exits. Perfection sounds like a lot of hard work for someone like you and me—and it is. Despite what you might have heard, this type of perfection, sanctification, is not the instant kind (that's justification). It's not like WHOOSH!! I'm living a perfectly obedient life. But why not? No, seriously; doesn't the Bible state that Believers, once they are justified, have everything they need for perfect obedience?

> *His divine power has granted to us all things that pertain*
> *to life and godliness, through the knowledge of him who*
> *called us to his own glory and excellence....*
>
> – 2 Peter 1:3 (ESV)

Hey, so let's get the WHOOSHin' started! Perfection, thy name is (fill in the Believer's name here). *Alas, it ain't that easy.* Remember that 50/50 Tobacco can? Believers have got a battle on their hands. However, it's not really the good half battling the bad half. As Peter states, Believers have everything. They're full. They are *justifiably* perfect.

No, the battle is not to do good, it's to fight our evil nature. Remember God puts it in, you work it out? Read, study, meditate, then do. All Believers have to do is clear the decks of their evil, worldly ways, and the Holy Spirit will use the Word of God to change them.

The beginning of perfection starts at reading God's word. If Believers do what they're supposed to do, the Holy Spirit does the rest.

> *"You must do what you can do, and then trust God to do what you can't."*
>
> – Joyce Meyers, Charismatic Christian author and speaker

It's a process. A from-second-to-minute-to-hour-to-day-to-week-to-month-to-year-growing-into-perfection process. It's the kind of perfection that is the product of failures, disappointments, frustrations, shame, conviction, successes, growth, and maturity.

In a nutshell, it's the perfection that's sorta like this:

> *And we all, with unveiled face, beholding the glory of the Lord, are being transformed into the same image from one degree of glory to another. For this comes from the Lord who is the Spirit.*
>
> – 2 Corinthians 3:18 (NASB)

As a Believer you will be taught patience and endurance, peace and joy, to be better prepared for whatever happens next in your life. You will be taught the perfection of obedience in order to be perfectly obedient. Yet, there is another reason The Teacher is preparing you to be an obedient slave: so you can teach others.

There's a kingdom coming; in fact, it's here. It's filled with obedient slaves to Jesus. You see, with the birth, death, and resurrection of Jesus Christ, a new government was created.

> *For a child will be born to us, a son will be given to us;*
> *And the government will rest on His shoulders.*
>
> – Isaiah 9:6 (NASB)

This government is a totally autocratic kingdom; there's one ruling King and all else are loyal, obedient subjects. The Kingdom of God is the kingdom, and Jesus Christ is King.

Jesus Christ as King

What does it mean that Jesus is King?

The main thrust of Jesus's teachings about the Kingdom of God were what it is like and when it would come. At the center of the Kingdom of God is a King— Jesus. When Jesus was arrested (John 18:33), Pilate asked him, "Are you the King of the Jews?" Jesus answered, "My kingdom is not of this world. If it were, my servants would fight to prevent my arrest by the Jewish leaders." Jesus here was identified as a king—but not the kind that Pilate knew.

Following a king is costly and requires submission: a surrender of will, coming under the authority of the king. Following a king is also beneficial because followers come under his protection and live in his provision.

The Kingdom of God will be established for the peace, prosperity, and welfare of the inhabitants. Jesus established His Kingdom in this world by his coming, secured it by His death, and will fully realize it upon His return.

Jesus the King has saved us from the penalty of sin through his death, is saving us from the power of sin through his indwelling presence, and will save us from the presence of sin through his return.

Jesus the King requires our submission and offers the benefit of redemption and entrance into his Kingdom of justice and joy, where sin can never reign over us.

– Nathan Foth

Movin' On Up.

> *"Well we're movin' on up (movin' on up)*
> *To the east side (movin' on up)*
> *To a deluxe apartment in the sky.*
> *Movin' on up (movin' on up)*
> *To the east side (movin' on up)*
> *We finally got a piece of the pie."*
>
> – theme song from *The Jeffersons, Movin' on Up*

> *"The kingdom of God is not coming with signs to be*
> *observed, nor will they say, 'Look, here it is!' or 'There!'*
> *for behold, the kingdom of God is in the midst of you.".*
>
> – Luke 17:20-21 (NASB)

"I don't wanna hear nothin' 'bout that Christian, you'll-understand-it-better-by-and-by, pie-in-the-sky stuff." You probably haven't heard it *quite* like that lately, but that's the way unsaved people (and some saved ones) spoke about the Kingdom of God. It was a place far, far, away, "up there…somewhere." But for Believers, the Kingdom of God is more than that. It's the endgame.

It's where Believers are to seek first (Matthew 6:33), have their citizenship (Philippians 3:20), keep their focus (Colossians 3:20), and where they will receive their inheritance (1 Corinthians 6:9). The Kingdom of God is a major part of the benefit of Christ as Lord, yet few Believers know what The Kingdom of God is, and even less find it beneficial. In order for you to get a better understanding of Christ as King, perhaps we should get a better picture of the kingdom, shall we?

The Kingdom of God (sometimes referred to as The Kingdom of Heaven) is here; at least that's what Jesus said. But the Jews didn't see the kingdom, even though they wanted to make Jesus king:

> *After the people saw the signs Jesus performed, they*
> *began to say, "Surely this is the Prophet who is to*
> *come into the world." Jesus, knowing that they intended*
> *to come and make him king by force, withdrew again*
> *to a mountain by himself.*
>
> — John 6:14-15 (NIV)

The Romans didn't see the kingdom, even though Pontius Pilate found out that Jesus was King of the Jews:

> *Therefore, Pilate said to Him, "So, you are a king?"*
> *Jesus answered, "You say correctly that I am a king. For*
> *this I have been born, and for this I have come into the*
> *world, to testify to the truth. Everyone who is of the truth*
> *hears My voice." Pilate said to Him, "What is truth?"*
>
> — John 18:37-38 (NASB)

Neither the Jews nor the Romans saw the kingdom when Jesus was crucified, even though the sign over His head stated He was king.

> *Pilate also wrote an inscription and put it on the cross.*
> *It was written, "JESUS THE NAZARENE, THE KING*
> *OF THE JEWS." Therefore many of the Jews read this*
> *inscription, for the place where Jesus was crucified was*
> *near the city; and it was written in Hebrew, Latin and in*
> *Greek. So the chief priests of the Jews were saying to Pilate,*
> *"Do not write, 'The King of the Jews'; but that He said, 'I*
> *am King of the Jews.'" Pilate answered, "What I have*
> *written I have written."*
>
> — John 19:19-22 (NASB)

So there seems to be agreement, at least between the Jews and the Romans, that Jesus claimed to be a king. So where's His kingdom? This question has been tripping up the Christian religion for two thousand years. Holy wars, Israel and the Middle East, American politics, civil rights, and the church all are asking, "Where is the kingdom?" Confused Christians want to know (or maybe not). As always, you who want to know something about God and His workings should go to the instruction manual, the Bible (2 Timothy 3:16-17). So let's gain a little profit and find out where the kingdom is according to the Bible.

Actually, there are *two* kingdoms: a spiritual and a physical. Let's start with the spiritual one. Jesus said that kingdom is inside you who believe (Luke 17:21). What does it mean that the Kingdom is in the midst of, or inside you? Remember this Kingdom is a spiritual kingdom? And what do all Believers have in common?

> *But you are not controlled by your sinful nature. You are*
> *controlled by the Spirit if you have the Spirit of God living*
> *in you. (And remember that those who do not have the*
> *Spirit of Christ living in them do not belong to him at all.)*
>
> – Romans 8:9 (NLT)

That Kingdom is a spiritual kingdom composed of those who have the Holy Spirit. How do you enter this Kingdom? Having Christ inside you provides you not only entrance, but citizenship.

Jesus Christ, the Son of God, by way of His Holy Spirit, is in the midst of and inside the Believer. What a coincidence that Believers are being shaped into the very image that is inside them! Makes it a lot easier to be conformed, don't you think? (More about that later in the chapter.)

What is most important right now is to know is that this Kingdom is a spiritual one, not yet a physical one. Why is this important? Because if you are going to be an obedient servant in this Kingdom, you must avoid those who have lost perspective, focus, or patience on the true kingdom. These are folks who want this spiritual kingdom to be a physical one TODAY!

Remember the Sea.

"When the ebbing tide retreats along the rocky shoreline,
it leaves a trail of tidal pools in a short-lived galaxy.
Each microcosmic planet a complete society.
A simple kind of mirror to reflect upon our own.
All the busy little creatures chasing out their destinies.
Living in their pools they soon forget about the sea...."

– Rush, *Natural Science*

Dear friends, I warn you as "temporary residents and
foreigners" to keep away from worldly desires that wage
war against your very souls.

– 1 Peter 2:11 (NLT)

The problem with Christians is they are still humans. They still have our five senses. They still have Earthly desires. They want to be comfortable, both physically and emotionally. They want what they want, when they want it, and how they want it. In short, humans long for situations to be *perfect*.

After all, being in a perfect state is the way God created us, all of us, at least according to the Book of Genesis (1:27 and 1:31). Although Man fell from this perfect state, he has longed to return to it. Christians, like any other humans, long for perfection, both within themselves and their environments (kinda like the Garden of Eden).

However, Believers must have an eternal, spiritual perspective. Once we've accepted Jesus Christ as Lord and Savior, the way we look at life changes…drastically (or it should). Just how much?

My desire is to depart and be with Christ, for that is far better.

– Philippians 1:23

For you folks who don't study languages, here's a clue: *depart* in this context means *die*. Dead, dirt nap, buy the farm, cash in your chips, bite the dust, …DEAD. Paul thinks he'd be much better off dead and being with Christ, although:

> **…it is more necessary for you that I remain in the body.**
> **Convinced of this, I know that I will remain, and I will**
> **continue with all of you for your progress and joy in the**
> **faith.**
>
> – Philippians 1:24-25 (NIV)

So, to paraphrase the passage, "I'd be better off dead than staying here on Earth. But because I love you guys, I'm gonna work with you to increase the satisfaction that comes from your faith." Now *that*, ladies and gents, is a kingdom-building perspective!

Heard any Christians talk like that lately? "When He's ready to take me, I'm ready to go?" Nah, me neither. More like *everybody wanna go to Heaven, but nobody wanna die*. You know, the kind of Christians whose team is in the Super Bowl and they wear their jerseys to church. (God forbid Jesus returns at the two-minute warning with the score tied!)

But you say, "not all Believers are like that," and you'd be right. Yet very few have a *heavenly* or *eternal* perspective. Very few keep their minds on things above and not things on the Earth as is commanded of them in Colossians 3:2. You know, the *pie-in-the-sky* point of view?

Unfortunately, Believers' fallen nature has caused them to be just a little impatient. Just as babies, we still want what we want, when we want it, and how we want it. Some fight this want better than others.

"Heaven can wait?" I think not! "And because I have no desire to die and be with Christ (in Heaven), I'll create a heaven here on Earth." Only this heaven is not the Kingdom of Heaven. It is an attempt to create a heaven based on Man's limited, impure understanding.

For I bear them witness that they have a zeal for God,
but not according to knowledge. For, being ignorant
of the righteousness of God, and seeking to establish
their own, they did not submit to God's righteousness.

– Romans 10:2-3 (ESV)

"In their own image, their world is fashioned. No wonder
they don't understand."

– Rush, *Natural Science*

Believers are here to expand the spiritual Kingdom of God on Earth, both internally (Philippians 2:12) and externally (Matthew 28:16-20). We have the King Himself inside us to guide us in our attempt. What a benefit! But by trying to move the spiritual Kingdom to this ethically challenged, morally corrupted, Earthly sewer, Believers can lose focus, perspective, and patience on the real work for real kingdom.

A Failure to Communicate.

"What we've got here is failure to communicate."

– Captain, *Cool Hand Luke* (1967)

My kingdom is not of this world. If my kingdom were of
this world, my servants would have been fighting, that I
might not be delivered over to the Jews. But my kingdom
is not from the world.

– John 18:36 (NASB)

WARNING: This section is going to make a lot of Christians upset. They'll get over it (or not). Jesus upset a lot of people. This section is long, and necessarily so, because you who are considering the value of Christ will miscalculate His benefit (and cost) if you agree with worldly views of the Kingdom. And now, *on with the show....*

Believers have, as their singular obligation, to do as Jesus would do. That's what it means to conform to His image, spiritual walk, maturing in Christ, following Christ...whatever religious saying floats your boat. Being like Christ means *being like Christ.*

If any of you remember the WWJD (What Would Jesus Do) bracelet craze, you know it burned out rather quickly. I have a theory on its sudden death. It wouldn't allow for Christians to do what they pleased, while pretending ignorance or obedience. No, if they wore such a reminder, then Christians would have to ask, "Would Jesus do this?" before they decided to sin. "Shoot, let me hurry up and take this bracelet off!!! Good, now where was I—oh that's right, sinning."

> ***Again Jesus spoke to them, saying, "I am the light of the world. Whoever follows me will not walk in darkness, but will have the light of life."***
>
> – John 8:12 (ESV)

> ***For everyone who does wicked things hates the light and does not come to the light, lest his works should be exposed.***
>
> – John 3:20 (ESV)

Thus, end of movement. Without a focus on Jesus and His Kingdom, Believers run off the rails, losing their perspective. And what, you ask, is that lost perspective? That Earth is not the home of the Believer (Hebrews 13:14) any more than that our citizenship is in our country of residency (Philippians 3:20). Believers need this point of view:

> *This is what the Lord Almighty, the God of Israel, says*
> *to all those I carried into exile from Jerusalem to Babylon:*
> *"Build houses and settle down; plant gardens and eat what*
> *they produce. Marry and have sons and daughters; find wives*
> *for your sons and give your daughters in marriage, so that they*
> *too may have sons and daughters. Increase in number there;*
> *do not decrease. Also, seek the peace and prosperity of the*
> *city to which I have carried you into exile. Pray to the Lord for it,*
> *because <u>if it prospers, you too will prosper</u> (emphasis added)."*
>
> – Jeremiah 29:4-7

Strangers and aliens (1 Peter 2:11), ambassadors of Christ (2 Corinthians 5:20). Folks, *We Believers live among you, but we're just passin' through, 'cause Babylon ain't our real home.* Or at least that's supposed to be the mindset of Believers. But a failure to communicate the truth appears. Let's look at two examples.

Whom would Jesus vote for? If He is focused on advancing His kingdom, which candidate will advance the Kingdom of God? *This group* votes because they long for Heaven on Earth (Matthew 6:10). The only problem is that the Kingdom is about souls, not lowering taxes. *And defendin' the Second Amendment ain't gonna make Jesus come back no sooner!* But no, say these Christians: *when we take over the gov'ment, then we can round up all the ungodly, and make it easier for when Christ finally shows up. Kinda helpin' the King out, sorta like.* (They fail to understand that "we have met the enemy, and it is us!" as we learned from the "Pogo" comic strip.) If someone could tell me which candidate will lead people to Christ, I'd stand in line until the Second Coming.

I heard my pastor preach another enlightened sermon a few Sundays ago— except one little, confusing part. To paraphrase, he said: I'm not telling you not to vote, just don't put your hope in it. Wha…wha...what?

So let me get this straight. Read both platforms, listen to speeches, read the position papers, watch the debates, pray over it (gotta throw some spirituality in this somewhere), stand in line for God knows how long, and then vote. Oh—but don't put any hope in the outcome of the election. This doesn't take the Believer's focus away from kingdom-building?

> *We must work the works of him who sent me while it is day;*
> *night is coming, when no one can work.*
>
> – John 9:4

And the work of Him who sent Jesus is not accomplished while wrapped in the flag!! Whoever's in this mindset doesn't understand that the love of Christ compels the Believer (2 Corinthians 5:14) to be of a people set apart for God's own use (1 Peter 2:9) and, therefore, they are not in need of Man's law, for the love of Christ and obedience to Him fulfills THE law (Romans 13:10). Pray tell me, political nationalistic, right-wing Christianity; is it the ***my kingdom*** part of John 18:36 that's confusing? But lest I be accused of political favoritism….

Jesus goes marching in a civil/social rights parade? Same concept from a different direction. These folks are committed to social justice/civil rights because they long for Heaven on Earth just as much. They are going to make us all so politically correct, so acutely aware of what annoys their "brothers and sisters" (not their kin in Christ, mind you, but humanity in general) that to tell humanity the truth (that they are sinners bound for Hell, but there's a way out through the forgiveness found in Jesus Christ) would cause a world-ending meltdown of the Earth's crust.

They do not understand that the truth changes people (John 14:6, John 17:17), that there can be no peace without truth (Luke 12:51-53), that God is the Great Discriminator (Ephesians 1:4-5), and that freedom can come only through Jesus (John 8:36, Romans 6:18).

How has drinking at the same water fountain, living in the same neighborhood, shopping at the same stores, eating in the same restaurants, attending the same schools, going to the same bathrooms (both racial and soon-to-be-gender neutral) brought one soul into the Kingdom? And speaking of the last point, do I really need to get started on the sexual orientation carousel?

To the political, social-gospel, left-wing Christianity; what does the *not of this world* section of John 18:36 mean? (*'Cause I be confused!*) Now stay with me here.

Please enlighten me, from either end of the aisle; has either of these perspectives brought *anyone* to the foot of Christ?

> ***What good is it for someone to gain the whole world,***
> ***yet forfeit their soul?***
>
> – Mark 8:36 (NIV)

The King Himself established the parameters of His kingdom by first stating what it is not. So even if all you rocket scientists out there on the right or the left don't know where the kingdom is, one thing is certain. **THE KINGDOM OF GOD IS NOT MADE UP OF THE SAME STUFF AS THIS WORLD!!!!**

That means, for those who got lost in the translation, that you cannot create, advance, or reach this Kingdom through worldly means! Not by voting, picketing, concealed carry, letters to the editor, social disobedience, fire-bombing, stockpiling guns, sit-ins, riots, or by wars (or rumors of wars), race- and/or socio-economic-baiting, or assimilation. Nada, zero, nothing. None of the world's devices can be used to enter or advance the Kingdom of God. Why?

Because—

> ***The person without the Spirit does not accept the things***
> ***that come from the Spirit of God but considers them***
> ***foolishness, and cannot understand them because they***
> ***are discerned only through the Spirit.***
>
> – 1 Corinthians 2:14 (NIV)

News flash; *it's a spiritual thang*. You're not going to find the Holy Spirit voting for politicians who wouldn't know Christ if they saw His wounds. And you won't find the King marching on Washington with a guy, Martin Luther King Jr. (no relation), who failed to openly confess (Romans 10:9) (1) Jesus was/is/will always be God (John 10:30-33), (2) Jesus's virgin birth (John 8:19), or (3) Jesus's resurrection from the dead (1 Corinthians 15:14-19). Would Jesus march with such a man (1 John 2:22-23)? Should the imitators of Christ?

Both these camps probably have good intentions, the building blocks of the road to Hell (Proverbs 14:12). Their impatience (or lack of want) for the physical Kingdom to come is surpassed only by the insufficiency (in satisfying whatever needs they have) of the present spiritual Kingdom. Like the Scripture says, they want a *type* of righteousness, a *good enough*.

Unknown to (or unacknowledged by) them is that the true righteousness they seek for this world can be had only through obedience to Jesus Christ. Nah, these guys will settle for good enough, a righteousness of their own making. They dilute the Good News, that Jesus can reconcile you to God, until it's unrecognizable. By trying to create their "heaven on Earth," both camps remind me of the beginning verses one of my favorite songs:

> *"God is great, God is good.*
> *He guards your neighborhood.*
> *Though it's generally understood;*
> *Not quite the way you would.*
> *You try to take the slack,*
> *stay awake and watch His back.*
> *But something happens every now and then,*
> *and someone breaks into the promised land."*
> — Jackson Browne, *Soldier of Plenty*

> *... as though He needed anything, since He Himself gives*
> *to all people life and breath and all things....*
> — Acts 17:25 (NASB)

They build their Earthly heaven with the help of the unbelieving world, as if that is what Jesus would do:

> ***Don't team up with those who are unbelievers.***
> ***How can righteousness be a partner with wickedness? How***
> ***can light live with darkness?***
>
> – 2 Corinthians 6:14 (NLT)

Christ does not need unbelievers to build His kingdom. In fact, by their very nature, the unbeliever's goals are the exact opposite of Christ's. They are not focused on obeying the King of kings (Revelation 19:16), but the prince of this world (John 12:31). In The Bondage of the Will, Martin Luther puts it like this:

> ***"Therefore, the Word of God, and the traditions of men, are***
> ***opposed to each other with implacable discord***
> ***(unstoppable disagreement); no less so, than God Himself***
> ***and Satan; who each destroy the works and overthrow the***
> ***doctrines of the other, as regal kings each destroying the kingdom***
> ***of the other."***

Let me make this simple: Christ is Lord over the Believer and the Unbeliever. He can get an Atheist to march for civil/social justice (and He does). He can get a God-Hater to "clean up the government" (and He does). But does the Unbeliever spread the Gospel? Does the Atheist bring the Good News to the world? Does the God-Hater tell Man He can be reconciled to God through Jesus Christ? Does the world expand the Kingdom of God? It's not an either/or thing, it's a matter of priority.

It's not about what Believers *can do*, it's about what Believers are here to do that *no one else can*. Jesus had a focus, what He had to do while he was on Earth (Luke 2:49, John 9:4, Luke 19:10). After all, isn't that why Believers are set apart in the first place, to do the work of the King (1 Peter 2:9)? In short, if *He* didn't focus on the world while He was on Earth, as imitators of Him, how do Believers do differently? Above all else, even food and water, Believers on Earth are to focus on the Kingdom of God (Matthew 6:33).

The litmus test for our good works in this world is as it states in the King's word:

> *Now Jesus did many other signs in the presence of the disciples, which are not written in this book; but these are written so that you may believe that Jesus is the Christ, the Son of God, and that by believing you may have life in his name.*
>
> *– John 20:30-31 (ESV)*

That's why Jesus performed good works; that Man might believe, to advance His kingdom. As imitators of Christ, the mission of the Believer is no less. Point those who think otherwise to these verses. People in the two camps we discussed do not fully benefit from Jesus Christ as King. For although they have been given the mind of Christ (1 Cor 2:16), they do not benefit from this insight to build His kingdom, and reduce their knowledge to the ignorance found in Unbelievers (Mark 4:11).

"Cake Is Good, Pie is Better."

> *"Agent T: Oh, good pie!*
> *Agent J: Oh, yeah. [T starts crying]*
> *Agent J: What's wrong, man? The pie not good?"*
>
> *– Men in Black II (2002)*

> *"The kingdom of heaven is like a mustard seed, which a man*
> *took and planted in his field. Though it is the smallest of*
> *all seeds, yet when it grows, it is the largest of garden plants*
> *and becomes a tree, …."*
>
> – Matthew 13:31-32 (NIV)

My wife, Marselene, LOVES pie. I'm a cake man myself, but Marselene always says "Cake is good; pie is better." That's the way to look at the "cake" of the physical world versus the "pie" of the physical Kingdom. There are enjoyable things in this world for Man. God created Eden for Man, and although the neighborhood has declined quite a bit, it still has its delights (Matthew 24:38, Jeremiah 29:5-6). That is, until you compare it to the Kingdom to come. So— what's up with this physical Kingdom?

The spiritual Kingdom is, eventually, going to grow into a physical one. Back in Jesus's day, there were only a few who believed. But the number grew as the disciples shared the message.

> *Yet many of the people believed in him.*
>
> – John 7:31 (ESV)

> *As he was saying these things, many believed in him.*
>
> – John 8:30 (ESV)

> *And many believed in him there.*
>
> – John 10:42 (ESV)

Ah, but some of you with sharp minds are asking, "How does this growing of the *spiritual* Kingdom of Believers create a *physical* one?" Glad you asked. You see, it all has to do with—time.

While a spiritual Kingdom is growing right under our very noses, God is readying the physical one. However, first things first. Jesus said that He has to get every soul that God the Father wills. All.

> *"All that the Father gives Me will come to Me, and the one*
> *who comes to Me I will certainly not cast out."*
>
> – John 6:37 (NASB)

Jesus has to get every soul that God the Father wills God the Son to have. This has to do with election. God has decided, through His right as God, who comes to Christ.

> *No one can come to Me unless the Father who sent*
> *Me draws him ....*
>
> – John 6:44 (NASB)

Now who those souls are, or how many of them there are, or when they will be born—that's in the Deuteronomy 29:29, known-to-no-one pile of knowledge. What we can glean from the Bible is that when all those who are supposed to come to Christ, to enter the spiritual Kingdom, come to Christ, that's when the party gets started (or is over, depending on your spiritual condition). I'm talking the end of the world as we know it—and the beginning of another world. We skipped a few steps in the creation of this physical kingdom. Why? Because many biblical scholars want to voice their opinion on the end times.

I have grown enough in *wisdom* to know I have not grown enough in *knowledge* to even attempt to argue with those great biblical minds on the subject of the end times. Like my momma always told me, "If you know, speak; if you don't know, shut up." Because I don't know the specifics, I'll have to stick with the mindset of Christ:

"Therefore be on the alert, for you do not know which day
your Lord is coming. But be sure of this, that if the head
of the house had known at what time of the night the thief
was coming, he would have been on the alert and would not
have allowed his house to be broken into. For this reason
you also must be ready; for the Son of Man is coming at an
hour when you do not think He will."

– Matthew 24:42-44 (NASB)

How about we settle on, not so much *when* He's coming back, but *that* He's coming back. This Earth is ending, and those who are in the spiritual Kingdom will be good to go. Okay? Okay. So that's the little clean-up about the structure of the kingdom. Just one more thing.

Morning is Here—Almost.

"By and by, when the morning comes,
When the saints of God are gathered home,
We will tell the story how we've overcome;
We will understand it better by and by."

– Charles Albert Tindley,
We'll Understand It Better By and By

Then I saw a new heaven and a new Earth; for the
first heaven and the first Earth passed away, and
there is no longer any sea.

– Revelation 21:1 (NASB)

What will this kingdom be like? Those in the spiritual Kingdom will then be a part of the physical kingdom in the new Heaven, I mean the new Earth, I mean…. The gang at *Gotquestions.org* provides a better definition than I ever could, so I'll just let them explain.

> *"Heaven—the new Earth—is a physical place where we will dwell with glorified physical bodies …. The concept that Heaven is "in the clouds" is unbiblical. The concept that we will be "spirits floating around in Heaven" is also unbiblical. The Heaven that believers will experience will be a new and perfect planet on which we will dwell. The new Earth will be free from sin, evil, sickness, suffering, and death. It will likely be similar to our current Earth, or perhaps even a re-creation of our current Earth, but without the curse of sin."*

Did you get that? "The new Earth will be free from sin, evil, sickness, suffering, and death." No wonder there are some who can't wait for Jesus to return and claim His rightful place as King of this new kingdom. And here's the kicker: Believers will be ruling right alongside Him! The Bible doesn't say: "Christ will fix this world and He needs the help of the Christian community to do it."

> *Do not love the world nor the things in the world. If anyone loves the world, the love of the Father is not in him. For all that is in the world, the lust of the flesh and the lust of the eyes and the boastful pride of life, is not from the Father, but is from the world. The world is passing away, and also its lusts; but the one who does the will of God lives forever.*
> — 1 John 2:15-17 (NASB)

This Earth will not need *anything* from the old Earth. In fact, the old Earth and ALL that is in it will be destroyed. It will pass away. So the work of the left and right leaning Christians, environmentalists, social justices, worldly peacemakers, and the whole lot, all will pass away. John MacArthur states is like this:

> **"From the remotest point of antiquity, men have dreamed of a golden age, they have longed for a utopia. They have written about it. They have desired an age of righteousness and an age of peace and an age when oppression would cease and injustice would be gone and war would end…. But it doesn't come until Jesus comes Himself."**

Ain't nothin' really happenin' 'til Jesus come back. That's why the Believer needs patience and perseverance today. *'Cause it might be a longgggggg wait.* In fact, if you're a Believer today, there's a better than even chance you might be dead and gone before Jesus comes back with His kingdom. That's why Believers build up the spiritual Kingdom today and wait for the return of Jesus tomorrow.

A thought comes to mind from my former pastor and still dear friend, Rev. Lorenzo Small. I once asked him about what we, as Believers, are supposed to be doing in the world. He said the world is the like the Titanic, and it's sinking. Our job is not to try and plug the hole, but get folks to the lifeboats. And that, my friends, is that. But what about the King?

Paid the Cost to Be the Boss.

> **"As long as I'm payin' the bills woman, I'm payin' the cost to be the boss."**
>
> – B.B. King, *Paying the Cost To Be The Boss*

> *"Worthy are You to take the book and to break its seals;*
> *for You were slain, and purchased for God with Your blood*
> *men from every tribe and tongue and people and nation.*
> *"You have made them to be a kingdom and priests to our*
> *God; and they will reign upon the Earth."*
>
> – Revelation 5:9-10 (NASB)

Jesus Christ is King. The whole spiritual Kingdom is His to command, now. And that spiritual Kingdom will be the foundation for the physical kingdom to come. But did you ever really think about what a king is?

king [kiNG]: a male ruler of a country who usually inherits

his position and rules for life

– Merriam-Webster Dictionary

Okay, not twenty questions, just two. What's a ruler? First, let's start with a rule.

rule \'rül\ : statement that tells you what is allowed or

what will happen within a particular system

– Merriam-Webster Dictionary

So a king is a man who dictates what is allowed and what will happen in his particular system, his kingdom. In short, *He's runnin' thangs*. He's the first and last word on everything. You might be too young to remember the bumper sticker that says:

> *"The Bible says it, I believe it, and that settles it."*

That sums up the Kingdom, except we no longer will have to read the instruction manual, the Bible, to figure out what Christ wants. As 1 Corinthians 13:12 (NLT) says:

Now we see things imperfectly, like puzzling reflections in a mirror, but then we will see everything with perfect clarity. All that I know now is partial and incomplete, but then I will know everything completely, just as God now knows me completely.

No more wondering if I'm doing *what* I'm supposed to be doing *when* I'm supposed to be doing it. No more attempting to fully understand the will of God through the Bible. No more getting my sanctification more wrong than right. Then I will know everything Jesus wants me to know because I will be everything He wants me to be, absolutely perfect, in every way, perfect. Perfect mind, perfect body, perfect spirit. I shall know and be known *fully*.

In the physical Kingdom, just like the spiritual one, Jesus will be in total and complete command. The king commands, and the subjects obey. Hey, doesn't this sound familiar? Uh, huh—of course! (I had to give you intellectuals out there time to reflect.) It's all about obedience!

I have heard it said that people in Hell would gladly take the opportunity to go to Heaven if they had it to do over. I don't understand that opinion. If you don't want to be obedient on Earth, for the limited time of your human lifespan, why would you want to be obedient—forever? There's an example of what I'm suggesting in the Book of Revelation.

Then the fifth angel poured out his bowl on the throne of the beast, and his kingdom became darkened; and they gnawed their tongues because of pain, and they blasphemed the God of heaven because of their pains and their sores; and they did not repent of their deeds.

– Revelation 16:10-11 (NASB)

The way I see it? *Just 'cause you don't want to go to Hell doesn't mean you want to go to Heaven.*

People who haven't been saved from the punishment, power, and presence of sin have nothing for which to be repentant, humbled, or happy. Their forever will not be among those who accepted the sacrifice of Jesus, who purchased those souls to place in His kingdom. They pledge no obedience, for they feel they have nothing on which to base their obedience.

> **So when we preach that Christ was crucified, the Jews are**
> **offended and the Gentiles (non-Jews) say it's all nonsense.**
> – 1 Corinthians 1:23 (NLT)

Those who do accept Jesus as Savior become obedient slaves to Him as Master, obedient students to Him as Teacher, and finally, obedient subjects to Him as King. It's a progression, a plan. It's *The Way*:

> **…that He who began a good work in you will perfect it**
> **until the day of Jesus Christ.**
> – Philippians 1:6 (NASB)

It's from glory to glory, through our obedience and His providence, that we become a perfect reflection of Jesus Christ, that the good work that Christ began at justification works through sanctification, and will conclude with glorification. That brings us full circle to the question that began this journey:

What shall you do with Jesus, who is called the Christ?

The Value of Christ:
Is He Worth It?

When I did consulting for small business owners, I'd often ask them why I should do business with them. They'd proudly rattle off a list of their products and services, their customer service and reliability. You know, all those things that would make doing business with them worth my time and money. However, there was one question that always caught them off guard: What if I don't need any of that?

The problem with selling something is an assumption that the person to whom you are selling needs it. The problem with spreading the Gospel in that mindset is, although every person needs the good news of Jesus Christ, it is not for everyone. Therefore, it's only valuable to those who think they need it.

Yeah, I know you might have heard differently, but let's think about salvation for a second. Let's start with John 3:16 (NIV):

> *For God so loved the world that he gave his one and only*
> *Son, that whoever believes in him shall not perish but have*
> *eternal life.*

But just like the question I asked the business owners: What if I don't need eternal life? In fact, what if I don't even *believe* in eternal life? How about if I don't believe in God nor His Son? In fact, what if I don't even believe the truthfulness of the book from which the verse was taken? Don't you think the value of Jesus Christ for that person would be...uh...well...next to nothing? Now we could take a look at this from Jesus's point of view:

> *For the Son of Man has come to seek and to save that*
> *which was lost.*

> – Luke 19:10 (NASB)

...Christ Jesus came into the world to save sinners...
$\qquad$ – 1 Timothy 1:15 (NASB)

"It is not those who are healthy who need a physician,
but those who are sick; I did not come to call the righteous,
but sinners."
$\qquad$ – Mark 2:17 (NASB)

"Come to Me, all you who are weary and burdened, and
I will give you rest."
$\qquad$ – Matthew 11:28 (HCBS)

Now if we just look at this thing from *Jesus's* point of view, perhaps we have a better understanding of who might be in need of His services:

- The lost, roaming the Earth in search of...something

- Those who acknowledge their disobedience and are sick with guilt

- Those who are spiritually weary and burdened

You see, folks, if you're on that list above, if you know you're wandering around this world in search of somewhere or something (or someone?) but can't find it, Jesus might be the guy for you. Or you might be aware that there is a God and you are consistently disobedient to Him, and you want to make it right. Or perhaps you are sick and tired (of being sick and tired...uh...no) of doing the same disobedient, stupid thing over, and over, and over.

Now these guys just might be in need of a Savior and a Lord. Jesus has a select group of people who will find Him valuable. (You can add to the list those found in Matthew 5:3-6.) And so—here we are. For a select group of people who know they have these particular needs, Christ might be the answer.

For others, like actor Stephen Fry (*V for Vendetta, Sherlock Holmes: A Game of Shadows, The Hobbit, Desolation of Smaug, The Hitchhiker's Guide to the Galaxy*, and a bunch more…)—not so much.

> *"'Why should I respect a capricious, mean-minded, stupid God*
> *who creates a world which is so full of injustice and pain?' That's*
> *what I'd say." Then, Byrne asks him whether he thinks he'd get*
> *in if he gave such an answer. "But I wouldn't want to! I wouldn't*
> *want to get in on his terms. They're wrong," Fry says.*
>
> – The Daily Beast, *Stephen Fry On What He'd Say To God*
> *At the Pearly Gates: "How Dare You"*

Ultimately, the value of Christ must be measured by a standard, either Satan's (and the world's) or that which God the Father has set. If your standard is the world's standard, *self*-realization, *self*-fulfillment, *self*-righteousness, *self*-love, *self*ishness (even when you do something for someone else, you don't give God the credit), — in short, *self* — then the benefit of Jesus Christ as Savior and Lord isn't worth the cost. Why? Because it will cost you everything, including your*self*, to fully benefit from Christ.

> *Yes, everything else is worthless when compared*
> *with the infinite value of knowing Christ Jesus*
> *my Lord. For his sake I have discarded everything*
> *else, counting it all as garbage, so that I could gain*
> *Christ.*
>
> – Philippians 3:8 (NLT)

On the flip side, if your goal is to be conformed to the image of God's Son, Jesus Christ, you will find the benefit of Christ as Savior and Lord infinitely greater than the cost. Why? Because that is how God designed salvation! (You know, like every product or service, it works best if *used as directed*?) And if you want what God wants, then you will get what God directed for you.

For the greatest value, the most benefit after the cost is considered, your new direction would need to be patterned after the image of Jesus. Then the rest of your existence will be based on one question: *What would Jesus do?* This is the basis for your joy now and your glory forever. The contemplation of this question in all that you think, say, and do will allow you to tap into the power that is within the Believer, gained through justification.

The Holy Spirit is in you to make you more like Christ. If you think *on* Christ, the Holy Spirit will help you think *like* Christ. In that moment, you will have the mind of Christ, and in His life is the joy of the union He had (and still has) with the Father.

> *"The glory which You have given Me I have given to them,*
> *that they may be one, just as We are one; I in them and*
> *You in Me, that they may be perfected in unity...."*
>
> –John 17:22-23 (NASB)

You can experience that joy now if you keep your mind on things above, and not things on the Earth.

> *Come close to God, and God will come close to you.*
> *Wash your hands, you sinners; purify your hearts, for*
> *your loyalty is divided between God and the*
> *world.*
>
> – James 4:8 (NLT)

Honor, praise, and — joy. Joy, because you're finally home, and boy, what a homecoming! Joy, because you did not suffer in vain. But this benefit of joy is only a component of the greater benefit of *glory*, to reign with Christ in His Kingdom.

glory glo·ry \ˈglȯr-ē\: public praise, honor, and fame
– Merriam-Webster Dictionary

> *But we should always give thanks to God for you,*
> *brethren beloved by the Lord, because God has chosen you*
> *from the beginning for salvation through sanctification by*
> *the Spirit and faith in the truth. It was for this He called*
> *you through our gospel, that you may gain the glory of our*
> *Lord Jesus Christ.*
> – 2 Thessalonians 2:13-14 (NASB)

That's right, ruling with Jesus in the Kingdom (Romans 8:17, 1 Corinthians 6:2-3, Revelation 3:21, Revelation 20:6). All that suffering and patience and perseverance; all that persecution and pain. All that *obedience*. All the cost of accepting Jesus Christ as Savior and Lord will seem petty compared to the ultimate benefit, glory.

What's the benefit after the cost of Jesus as Savior and Lord is obedience through sacrifice? When it's all said and done, when you've fought the good fight, finished the race, and kept the faith, you should expect a crown (2 Timothy 4:7-8) and with it—glory. Glory comes at the cost of obedience. And this is the final value equation:

The Value of Christ = Eternal Glory – Eternal Obedience

This is the equation of God to return Man to the desired state (Genesis 1:26) and the relationship he had with God in the Garden of Eden—only better. A return to a glorious relationship with God, the benefit of glory at the cost of obedience is the true value of Christ.

So, having all the facts, and choosing a standard from which to judge benefit and cost, what is the value of Christ — to you?

Epilogue

Thank you for sticking it out. It's been a ride, both for me writing this book, and I'm sure for you reading it. It was never meant to evangelize; it was merely meant to inform. God does not sell, He's more of supply-side economist. *If you build it, they will come*, like it says in John 12:32.

My prayer is that you now have a clearer understanding of the value of Jesus Christ as a personal Savior and Lord. It took *me* a while to get with *His* program. I'm still somewhat of a disobedient slave; but it's, you know, from glory to glory.

Finally, I leave you with these thoughts:

"If it is disagreeable in your sight to serve the LORD,
choose for yourselves today whom you will serve: whether
the gods which your fathers served which were beyond the
River, or the gods of the Amorites in whose land you are
living; but as for me and my house, we will serve the
LORD."

– Joshua 24:15 (NASB)

Let us therefore, as many as are perfect, have this attitude;
and if in anything you have a different attitude, God will
reveal that also to you; however, let us keep living by that
same standard to which we have attained.

– Philippians 3:15-16 (NASB)

"So I'll cherish the old rugged Cross,
till my trophies at last I lay down.
I will cling to the old rugged Cross,
and exchange it some day for a crown."

– George Bennard, *The Old Rugged Cross*

Look for the next book, *Now What? Christlikeness and the Imperfect Pursuit of Perfection,* available, Lord willing, December, 2017. Go to www.John442.com for more details.

Ever Forward.